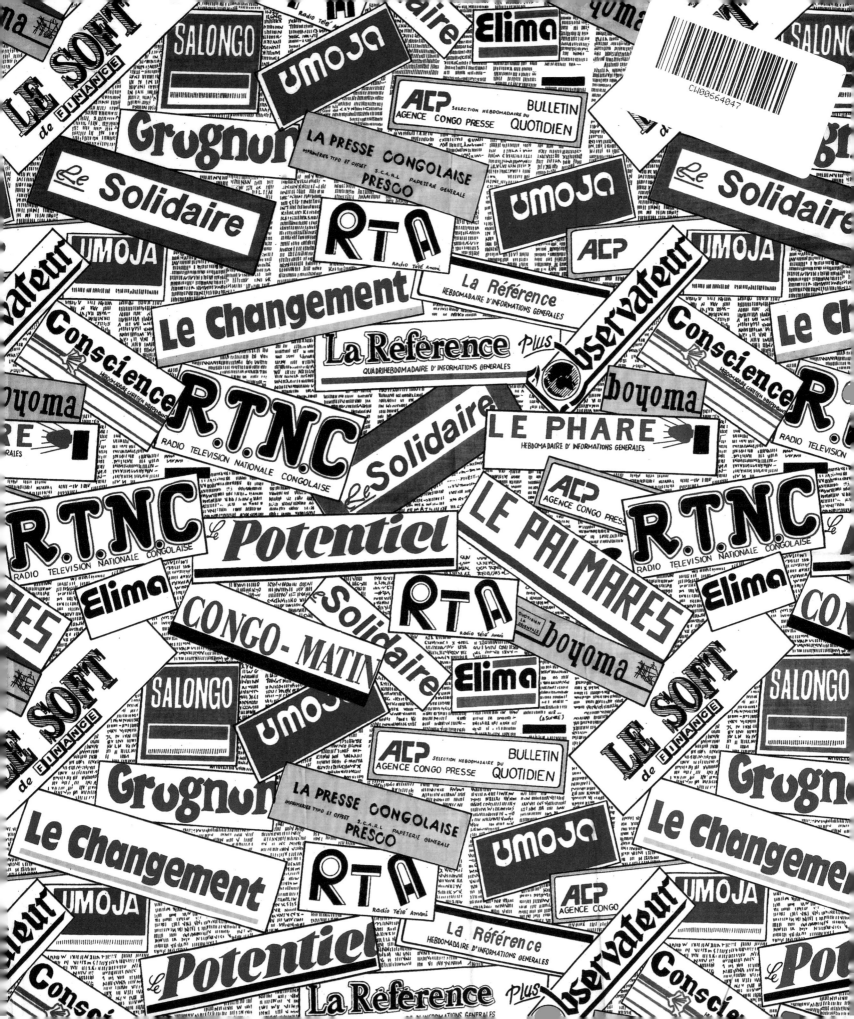

AFRICAN TEXTILES TODAY

CHRIS SPRING

AFRICAN TEXTILES TODAY

CHRIS SPRING

THE BRITISH MUSEUM PRESS

This book is dedicated to John Picton.
JP's exhibitions and publications, together with his generously
shared knowledge and wisdom, are an ongoing inspiration to
all who love African textiles.

This book is also written in memory of Claude Ardouin
and Cordelia Obiageli Banks, 'Delia'.
Claude and Delia, in their very different ways, were closely
connected to the British Museum and shared a passion for
the textile traditions of Africa. They are sorely missed.

First published in 2012 by The British Museum Press
A division of The British Museum Company Ltd
38 Russell Square
London WC1B 3QQ
britishmuseum.org/publishing

A catalogue record for this book is available from the
British Library

ISBN: 978-0-7141-1559-7

Designed by Paul Palmer-Edwards at Grade Design
Printed and bound in China by Toppan Leefung Printing Ltd

The papers used by the British Museum Press are recyclable
products and the manufacturing processes are expected to conform
to the environmental regulations of the country of origin.

Frontispiece Young Sotho men wearing their post-initiation
blankets, *lekhokolo*. From the series *A New Beginning* by Araminta
de Clermont. Cape Town, South Africa, 2009–10 (*see* p. 228 for
full caption).

The African textile collection of the British Museum

The British Museum's collection of African textiles stands at just
under 4,500 pieces. A large portion of the collection originates
from West Africa, although there are also significant holdings
of northern, eastern, central and south-eastern African textiles.
They range from hand-woven raffia cloths from Sir Hans
Sloane's bequest of 1753 – the Museum's founding collection –
to industrially manufactured fabrics of the twenty-first century.
In addition, the Museum holds numerous textile-related objects
such as looms, weaving combs, stencils, printing blocks and
templates for machine-printed cloth. The majority of the Museum's
collection was acquired as a result of anthropological fieldwork
backed up by meticulous documentation.

The collection reflects the global impact of African textile
traditions, as well as the assimilation and transformation of textile
traditions from around the world by African cultures, tastes and
patronage. Most significantly, the Museum's collection includes a
growing number of works, in a variety of media, by contemporary
artists of African heritage informed or inspired by long-established
African textile traditions.

Contents

The global phenomenon of African textiles

One of the most obvious facts about West Africa is that there is a lot of cloth around.[1]

JOHN PICTON

Walk round any market in Marrakesh, Dar Es Salaam, Johannesburg or in any town or village in northern, eastern or southern Africa, and the same fact will rapidly become apparent. Textiles – whether hand-woven, factory-printed, resist-dyed, stamped or embroidered – are arguably the most obvious visible signifier of culture throughout the African continent, or for that matter wherever in the world people of African descent have settled. The history, beliefs, fashions, status and aspirations of people may be read through the colours and patterns of textiles, the means and materials by which and from which they are made, and the occasions on which they are worn or otherwise utilized.

Drawing on recent research by staff at the British Museum, and the Museum's fine collection of African textiles, this book attempts to give a selective overview of the innumerable textile traditions of Africa, as well as an insight into how they have inspired and informed the work of contemporary artists and photographers. A few of these traditions are described in this introduction, and will be examined in greater detail later in the book.

A welcome and a warning: *kangas* of eastern Africa

We begin with a welcome and a warning. The first message is unequivocal, the second far more enigmatic, but each is delivered through the medium of textiles known as *kanga*, widely worn by women (and sometimes by men) in eastern Africa. Both textiles are factory printed, one produced in Kenya, the other in India; both have inscriptions in Kiswahili printed on them: KARIBU MGENI, 'Welcome stranger' and HUJUI KITU, 'You know nothing'. The first *kanga* was

Printed cloth (*kanga*)
Cotton
Kenya, early 21st century
110 x 169 cm
British Museum, 2011,2002.56

The inscription reads:
'Welcome stranger'.

Printed cloth (*kanga*)
Cotton
Tanzania, early 21st century
105 x 154 cm
British Museum, Af2002,09.4

The inscription reads:
'You know nothing'.

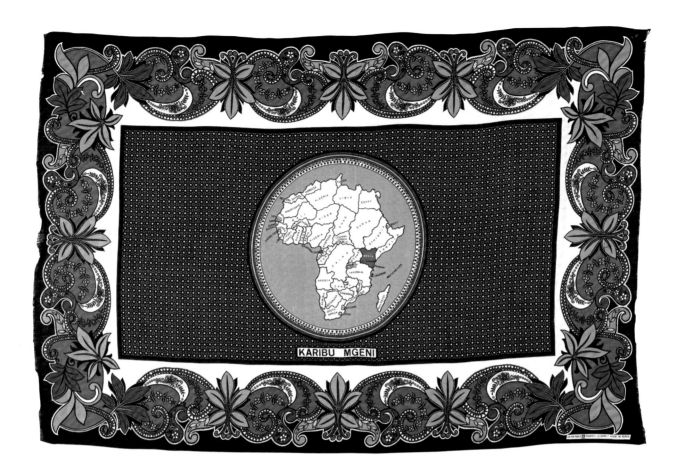

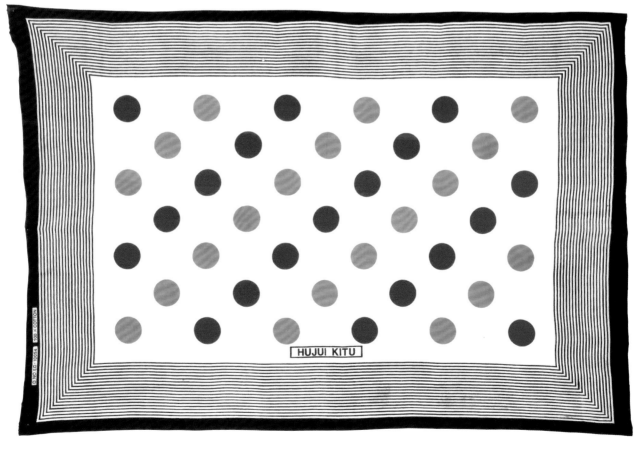

purchased in the Kenyan port of Mombasa, the other in another ancient port, Zanzibar town in Tanzania. The wearing of printed cloth by women in eastern Africa was initially a powerful symbol of emancipation[2] (slavery was not officially abolished in this region of Africa until 1897) and the inscriptions in Kiswahili which increasingly appeared on them are a means of communicating ideas which might be difficult or impossible to say out loud. For example, *hujui kitu*, 'You know nothing', is a message which might be worn by an older woman to comment on her younger rivals – or whoever might represent a threat to her in one way or another.

I have come as a stranger to many countries in Africa and I have always been welcomed with great warmth, hospitality and generosity. I have also always come with a mindset of *hujui kitu*, because if I know nothing I may begin to learn something, but if I think I know everything, I will never learn anything.

Tent-makers of Cairo

Another textile greeting and warning comes from the north in the great city of Cairo. The textile is created by the hand of a modern master, Salah El Din M. El Ozy, a practitioner of the ancient tradition of the *khiyamiya* or tent-makers of Cairo. Such cloths are painstakingly formed through a process of drawing designs on a canvas base, onto which coloured sections of cloth are sewn in a method known as appliqué. Historically, large tents or *siwan* formed the beginnings of the city long before any solid buildings were constructed, welcoming those who had crossed the desert from the lands to the south, east and west. Today, temporary tents are often created in Cairo's streets using lamp posts as a framework; they are erected for a variety of important events, including weddings, funerals and religious celebrations. For centuries these tents included inscriptions around their entrances, thoughts for the guests to ponder, and El Ozy uses the words of the ninth-century poet and philosopher Diwan Abu Nawas to deliver his own personal message: 'Say it to one who knows it all. You might have learned something, but many things have passed you by'.

Interestingly enough, this textile and the '*hujui kitu*' kanga (see p. 7) were both displayed at the entrances to pioneering exhibitions: *Textiles, Tradition*

Doorway/tent-hanging by Salah El Din M. El Ozy
Cotton, canvas
Egypt, late 20th century
387 x 376 cm
British Museum, Af1998,08.1

The inscription above the doorway reads: 'Say it to one who knows it all. You might have learned something, but many things have passed you by.'

Inset Street in Cairo with tent-hangings.

فَقُلْ لِمَنْ يَدَّعِي فِي الْعِلْمِ فَلْسَفَةً ۞ حَفِظْتَ شَيْئًا وَغَابَتْ عَنْكَ أَشْيَاءُ

and Lurex at the Barbican Art Gallery, London in 1995[3] and *Hazina: Traditions, Trade and Transitions in Eastern Africa* at the Nairobi Gallery, Kenya, in 2006.[4]

Communicating through cloth: Tanzania, Mozambique and Ghana

In southern Tanzania and particularly in Mozambique, the printed textiles worn by women are known as *capulana* and have a similar significance and usage to *kanga* in eastern Africa. Among the Makonde people a female masquerade, *lingundumbwe*, was created in the 1970s using *capulana* and *kanga*, partly as a means of declaring female power and authority, but also as a more public alternative to a much older and highly secretive tradition of masquerade using ceramic masks.[5] Female characters are frequently depicted in African masquerade but, with very few exceptions, the masqueraders themselves are men. Despite the objections of Makonde men, whose *mapiko* masquerade involves the wearing of a wooden helmet mask, Makonde women invented their own mask made of *capulana* wrapped around a cardboard frame. Men were initially enraged at what they saw as the usurpation of a male preserve by women. In response Makonde women pointed to the vital part that they – initially inspired by Josina Machel (the wife of the future president Samora Machel) – had played in the war of independence against the Portuguese colonial power, an argument which found great sympathy among the members of the government in Maputo.

Travelling across the continent to the Asante kingdom of Ghana in West Africa, we encounter another means of embellishing cloth. The ancient tradition of hand printing the many different *adinkra* symbols onto cloth, using stamps carved from sections of gourd, finds an ever-increasing market despite – as is the case with the Egyptian tent-makers and most other handmade cloths in Africa – competition from factory-made versions. *Adinkra* is an Akan word which describes the process of 'saying farewell to the dead' and it was in this context that *adinkra* symbols were first used. Each *adinkra* symbol is named and has a rich variety of nuanced meaning, which contributes to the wonderfully sophisticated means of communication developed by the Akan peoples of Ghana.

Above left and right Makonde *lingundumbwe* cloth masquerade costume. This masquerade took place near Dar Es Salaam in Tanzania; the dancer uses both *kanga* and *capulana* in her costume.

Adinkra cloths may be worn on many important occasions, though varieties worn at funerals are normally dyed blue or red.

In 1991, while digging the foundations for a skyscraper in downtown Manhattan, workers came across the remains of some of the 20,000 enslaved Africans who had initially been brought by the Dutch to New Amsterdam in 1626, and after 1664 by the British, to build the city which would become New York. Many of these men, women and children were identified as coming from the region of modern-day Ghana, one in particular by the pattern of an *adinkra sankofa* symbol still recognizable on the remains of his coffin.[6] Following a sustained campaign, work on the skyscraper was halted until a number of remains had been respectfully re-buried on the site and a marble monument erected, on the walls of which a number of *adinkra* symbols are engraved (see p. 12).

For all those who were lost
For all those who were stolen
For all those who were left behind
For all those who were not forgotten

Reading history through textiles

The 'Middle Passage' of the transatlantic slave trade, which took millions of enslaved Africans to the Americas and the Caribbean, also spread numerous African traditions in music, language and art, along with the religious beliefs that informed these practices. These cultural memories helped to fuel the resistance and rebellion of enslaved African peoples, including the uprising in Santo Domingo (today the Republic of Haiti) led by Toussaint L'Ouverture in 1791, which ultimately led to abolition and emancipation.

Some of this history may be traced in the migration of symbols used in the patterning of cloth, and may still be read today all over the world. A nineteenth-century appliqué banner celebrating King Glèlè of Dahomey (today the Republic of Benin) depicts the king in divine aspect in the guise of a number of gods, including the warrior Daghesu and the androgynous, one-legged

African Burial Ground, New York City. The *sankofa* symbol on the monument exhorts us to 'learn from the past so that we may live a better life in the present'.

Hand-stamped *adinkra* cloth with narrow strips of *kente*
Cotton, silk
Asante people, Ghana,
early 20th century
199 x 310 cm
British Museum, Af1936,1211.5,
donated by Captain Robert P. Wild

creator god Mawu-Lisa of the Fon people, holding the moon in one hand and the sun in the other (see p. 15). These gods, *vodun*, form the basis of the pantheon of deities at the heart of the voodoo religious practices of Haiti and the embroidered *drapo* or flags used by their followers.[7] This symbol of Daghesu and Mawu-Lisa, in stylized form, has today made its way onto the door of the gents' toilet in a bar on Fuerteventura, one of the Canary Islands, which became an entrepôt for enslaved Africans bound for the Caribbean from West Africa on the Middle Passage (see p. 15). Today that trade has been reversed, as hundreds of thousands of African economic migrants make the perilous journey to the islands of the Atlantic and Mediterranean seeking a new life in Europe. The nineteenth-century textile and its portrayal of the king/god left its mark in the twenty-first century in a place and context which is very different – and yet is undoubtedly part of that ongoing history.

Followers of Osun, a Yoruba *orisha* or deity who is the guardian of every person's inner soul, at the annual festival, Osogbo, Nigeria, 2007. They wear dresses of imported lace and wax-printed cloth.

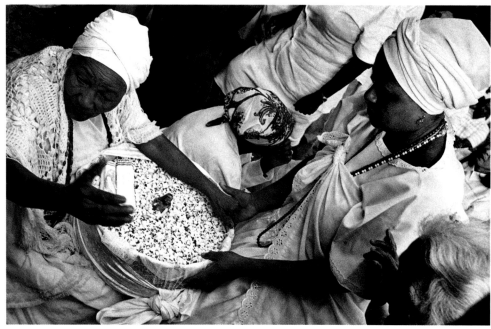

Followers of Omolu – the complex deity who can bring disease but can also protect from illness – better known in Nigeria as Xapanã. Salvador, Bahia, Brazil, 2007. Their dress echoes styles worn by Portuguese women of the 18th century.

Image of Mawu-Lisa on the door of the gents' toilet in a bar on Fuerteventura, Canary Islands, 2011.

Appliqué banner celebrating King Glèlè of Dahomey
Cotton
Fon people, Republic of Benin,
19th century
175 x 109 cm
British Museum, Af1982,23.1

Textiles and trade:
four stories from global Africa

It is impossible to discuss African textiles without recognizing the central importance of trade – local, regional, long-distance and intercontinental – in the development of almost all traditions across time and place. In many parts of the world today we may encounter a variety of African textile traditions without necessarily being aware of their historical roots among the (often very small) groups of people who originally created and/or used these cloths. I will briefly trace four such traditions and their ongoing global impact.

Ethiopia and the Indian Ocean 'Silk Road'

Our first story begins in the mid nineteenth century among the Christian noblewomen of the central and northern highlands of Ethiopia. These women wore tunics probably made of imported cotton sheeting (as likely as not manufactured in Manchester, UK), but which they embroidered around the neck and sleeves with complex and colourful patterns created from imported Chinese silk. Just as the overland Silk Road had brought this precious material from China across Central Asia to Europe and the Middle East, so the trade winds created a watery 'road' for silk and other textiles across the Indian Ocean to eastern Africa, a trade which continues to this day. One of the highest offices in the courts of the great Ethiopian kings and emperors was the Keeper of the Silk Caves, overseeing the cool, dark and moist environment that provided the ideal storage place for the vast quantities of raw Chinese silk used in creating garments, accoutrements and wall hangings for the complex hierarchies of church, army and state. Today, well-to-do Christian women in Ethiopia wear a version of this nineteenth-century dress, but the original pattern and variants, usually factory-printed, are worn by men and women all over the world as a signifier of global Africa.

Noblewoman's tunic
Cotton, silk
Ethiopia, 19th century
110 x 167 cm
British Museum, Af,Ab.1

June Bam-Hutchison, wearing an 'Ethiopian' patterned dress, greets Erroll Hendricks at the South African High Commission, 2011.

'Kasai velvet' from the southern Congo Basin

Our next story comes from central Africa, from the southern tributaries of the great Congo River basin and, in particular, the raffia palm-leaf textiles of the Kuba and other peoples of this region. Some of these textiles were embroidered with a particular method known as 'cut-pile', using a special knife to cut each thread of raffia as it is drawn through the base cloth, thus creating a surface texture similar to velvet. In the early twentieth century the author Joseph Conrad set his novella *Heart of Darkness* in this part of Africa. Conrad's work created in the European imagination a vivid image which strongly reinforced notions of the primitive savagery of the so-called 'Dark Continent'. Yet the spectacular art of the peoples living in this part of Africa, including luminous textiles in a dazzling array of patterns and colours, seemed to tell another story.

Two exhibitions of this art, staged in London and New York in the early twentieth century, began to alter Western perceptions for those who wished to see beyond the stereotypes. The collections made by Emil Torday and displayed at the British Museum[8] had a powerful impact on contemporary artists of the

Cut-pile embroidered cloth
Raffia
Kuba-Ngongo people, Democratic Republic of Congo, early 20th century
61.5 x 76 cm
British Museum, Af1979,01.3177

time, as did a massive exhibition curated by Stewart Culin at the Brooklyn Museum, New York (where it also fed the emerging Harlem Renaissance).[9] The Brave New World of twentieth-century Europe had been brought to a terrible halt by the First World War, and now the worlds of fashion and design looked to Africa for inspiration – and have been doing so ever since.

The idea that 'fashion' and haute couture are purely European or Western inventions is nonsense. Even in the 1920s, Europeans were simply appropriating designs which were already 'fashionable' in Africa – in the late nineteenth century, Zanzibar was known as the 'Paris of eastern Africa'.[10] Today, African fashion designers are leading the world in the variety and imaginative breadth of their creations, yet top designers such as Oumou Sy of Senegal proudly maintain their African identity and help to inspire the rapidly growing fashion industry in various parts of the continent. Meanwhile, a visit to the Shabazz Harlem Market in New York will give an inkling of how many designs and fashions for peoples of African descent around the world find their roots in the textile traditions of Africa.[11] One tradition, that of the *bogolanfini* or 'mud cloths' of the Bamana people of Mali, is the inspiration behind a global industry which is visible in a vast array of garments, accoutrements and upholstery.[12] It is also the subject of our next story.

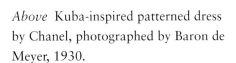

Above Kuba-inspired patterned dress by Chanel, photographed by Baron de Meyer, 1930.

Right Art Deco sofa of the early 20th century with upholstery inspired by Kuba-Ngongo textiles.

Mud cloths of Mali

In common with Kuba cut-pile raffia textiles, the base cloth for *bogolanfini* is woven by men and subsequently decorated by women, using entirely locally sourced materials, though that is where the similarity ends. The cotton base cloth of *bogolanfini* is created in a distinctively West African technique known as narrow-strip weaving, in which individual strips of cloth are sewn together to make a larger textile. This cloth is then 'discharge' dyed by women using a combination of river mud and a caustic solution in a process which in many ways is the reverse of the much more widespread technique of resist-dyeing. The complex patterns thus produced are thought to conceal a coded system of meaning with a variety of protective and beneficial properties.[13] The cloth itself is worn as a wrap-around skirt by married women and, in tailored versions, by men, particularly hunters, who wear it in the form of tunics, caps and trousers. Historical events are frequently recorded by the naming of cloth, as in the example below in which a battle between the nineteenth-century warlord Samory and the French colonial forces is commemorated.

Not far from Bamana country in Mali, in the lands now occupied by the Dogon people, some of the most ancient textiles ever discovered in sub-Saharan Africa were excavated in burial caves in the Bandiagara escarpment,[14] though many of these textiles were created using techniques such as narrow-strip

Furniture upholstered with 'mud cloth' pattern, Oliver Tambo International Airport, Johannesburg, South Africa.

Narrow-strip cotton textile (*bogolan*)
Cotton, mud and vegetable dye
Bamana people, Mali, late 20th century
87 x 130 cm
British Museum, Af1987,07.18

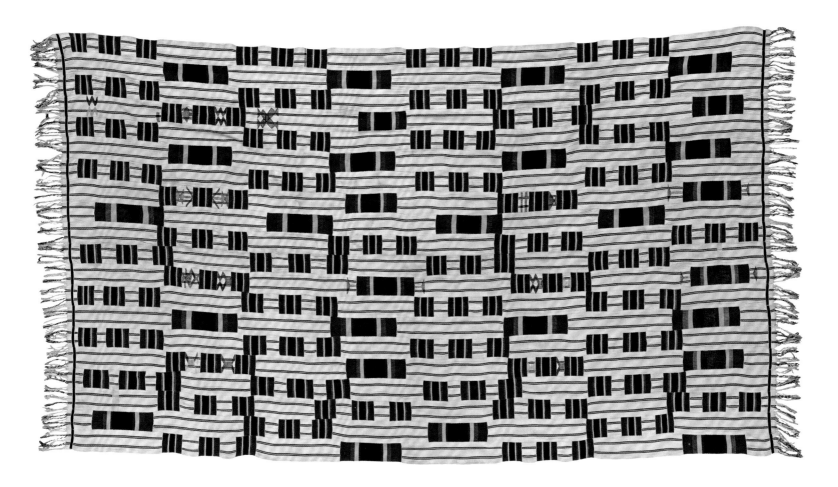

Narrow-strip textile
Cotton
Ewe people, Ghana, mid 20th century
159 x 402 cm
British Museum, Af1955,05.252, donated
by Miss M. Best

Jasper Conran 'Ewe' sofa, The Conran
Shop, London, 2011.

weaving still widely practised today. The variety of different types of cloth
found there, some dating back to the ninth century AD, bear witness to the
ancient caravan trade in cloth across the Sahara, from North Africa to the
Sahel and further south down the great river systems of the Niger to the
forested coastal regions of the Gulf of Guinea.

Kente cloth of Ghana

Up to now this introduction has looked at some of the traditions which are
very much 'African', but which may not necessarily be immediately
recognizable as such to many Westerners. For the fourth story in the sequence,
we turn to something that in many ways epitomizes the popular notion of an
'African textile': the great narrow strip hand-woven cloths of West Africa, in
particular to the famous *kente* cloths of the Ewe and Asante people of Ghana.
The term *kente* has become a global catch-all used to describe the silk narrow-
strip cloth of the Asante and Ewe people in particular, though its origins may
lie in its historical use by Fante traders to describe the silk cloths they had
purchased in the Asante capital Kumase. In common with all the other

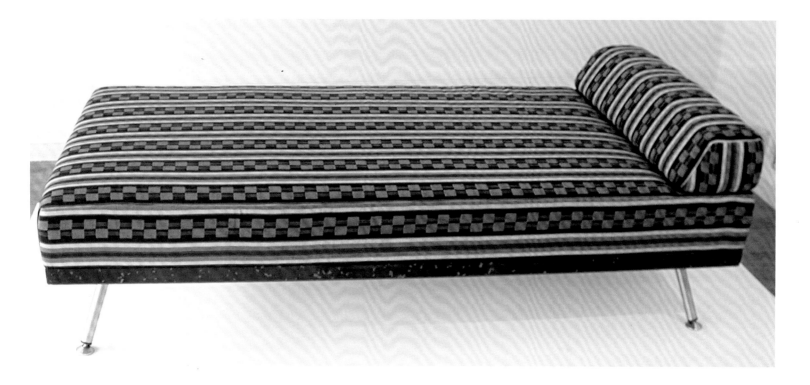

traditions featured in this introduction, the early *kente* cloths were worn by a very small and select group of people. In the case of the Asante, silk narrow-strip cloth was a royal monopoly, to be worn only by the *Asantehene* (king) and other members of the royal court in Kumase. Today, versions of *kente*, whether hand-woven or machine-printed, may be found all over the world and, just like the other textiles in our four stories, *kente* designs have found their way onto upholstery and curtain fabric, as well as onto every conceivable item of dress. Many of the familiar patterns of London Transport (now Transport for London) upholstery, particularly those designed by Enid Marx for the London Passenger Transport Board in the 1930s,[15] were clearly inspired by *kente* cloth, a fact which the artist Taslim Martin celebrates in some of his own creations[16] (see above).

Arguably the most remarkable and visually stunning of the many creations which, in one way or another, have the leitmotif of *kente* at their core are the magnificent sculptures by the artist El Anatsui, using the metal foil wrappers found around the necks of liquor bottles. From this unlikely material the artist has created sculptures that have put him among the most renowned of all contemporary artists – and at the heart of an understanding of these remarkable sculptures lies the profound significance that surrounds the making, naming, using and wearing of cloth in Africa.[17]

Above **Kente Day Couch** by Taslim Martin, 2007. Upholstery, stainless steel and recycled plastic.

Right **Woman's Cloth** by El Anatsui
Metal foil
Nsukka, Nigeria, 2002
287 x 292 cm
British Museum, Af2002,10.2

Football and cloth in Africa

Africa's economic, technological and cultural renaissance has been ignored in much of the West. The continent is still known more for its dictators and rebels than for its entrepreneurs and artists. But since Cameroon's triumph in 1990 there is one other thing that Africa has become known for, though: football.[18]

STEVE BLOOMFIELD

Bloomfield was writing in advance of the 2010 FIFA World Cup in South Africa, and his hope that the competition would show Africa in a more positive light has been largely vindicated, despite – or perhaps because of – the renewed focus on rebels and dictators which the 'Arab Spring' of 2011 inevitably provided. Long a popular sport, football is an increasingly important factor in African life and politics and is also providing African players and the countries they represent with a positive global profile. African textile traditions, always a barometer for popular taste and opinions in Africa, inevitably reflect this powerful current, as do Africa's artists.

Above **Printed cloth commemorating the 2010 FIFA World Cup**
Cotton
South Africa, 2010
108 x 282 cm
British Museum, 2011,2019.3

Left **Printed cloth celebrating the 'Indomitable Lions of Cameroon' and their participation in the 2002 FIFA World Cup in Korea and Japan**
Cotton
Cameroon, 2002
119 x 182 cm
British Museum, 2011,2002.12

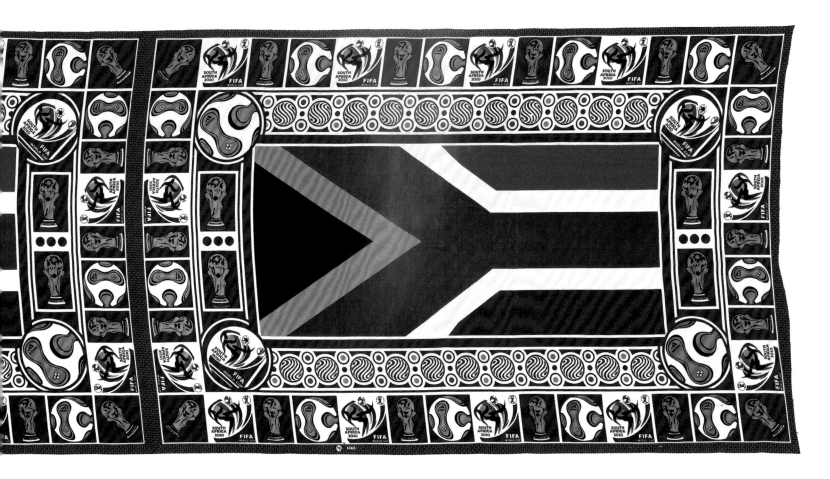

Nike v Adidas **by Hassan Hajjaj, 2010**
(AH **1431**)

The artist/designer/photographer Hassan Hajjaj uses cloth in a variety of humorous installations, which, nonetheless, have very serious points to make. Using 'the universal language of sport', Hajjaj looks at stereotypical notions of Morocco and North Africa, which have their roots in European Orientalist images of the nineteenth century, bringing them up to date with a combination of his own skill as a designer and photographer. He creates his own versions of the hooded gowns (*djellaba*) and face-veils (*niqab*), so often demonized in the West, and playfully appropriates the branding of internationally famous sports goods manufacturers such as Nike and Adidas to dress his models.

In common with Nike and Adidas (see p. 25), Manchester United is a global brand. It is no coincidence that the printed bandanas created in Ghana to celebrate M.U.F.C and Asante Kotoko F.C. are similar in design and colour, perhaps in the hope that some of the Manchester club's star quality might rub off on their Kumase cousins – or vice versa, if you happen to be a Kotoko fan.

The printed cloths, *kanga*, with which this chapter began, would seem a fitting way in which to draw it to a close. The images and the Kiswahili slogans on these cloths provide an unspoken language through which women in eastern Africa converse with one another and with the men in their lives.[19] A very popular design produced in the Urafiki ('Friendship') textile company, in Dar Es Salaam in 2002, shows an image of the main football stadium on Zanzibar together with the inscription MCHEZA KWAO HUTUZWA, 'He who plays at home shall be rewarded', a clear message from women to their husbands or boyfriends to 'play away' at their peril (see pp. 28–9).

Printed Manchester United F.C. bandana
Cotton
Ghana, 2006
51 x 50 cm
British Museum, Af2006,12.14

Printed Asante Kotoko F.C. bandana
Cotton
Ghana, 2006
53 x 51 cm
British Museum, Af2006,12.13

MCHEZA KWAO HUTUZ

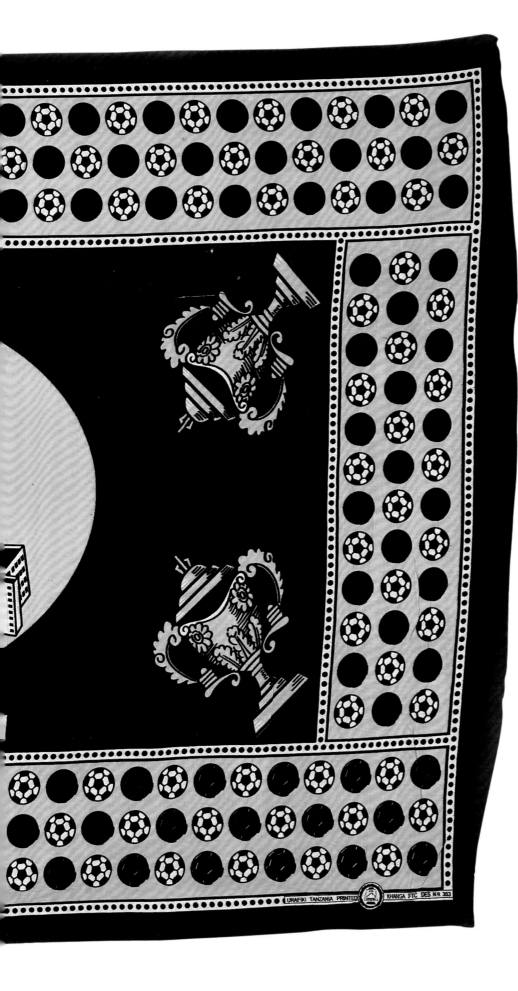

Printed cloth (*kanga*)
Cotton
Tanzania, 2002
112 x 167 cm
British Museum, Af2002,09.12

The inscription reads: 'He who plays at home shall be rewarded'.

AFRICAN TEXTILES AS HISTORICAL DOCUMENTS

Tablet-woven church hanging (detail)
Silk
Gondar, Ethiopia, mid 18th century
306 x 63 cm
British Museum, Af1868,1001.22

This panel shows King Bakaffa of Ethiopia
(d. 1730) flanked by angels. It was woven,
probably by Jewish tablet-weavers from
the Yemen, using imported Chinese silk.
(See p. 41 for full caption.)

African textiles as historical documents

You know you can memorialize a lot of things in cloth instead of having a statue in bronze or marble; in fact, these days cloth is loaded with so much meaning that it is rare to go to a cloth market, for instance, and find a cloth which does not have a name. And the name is not something which has come out of the blue, it's something tied to that place or a person or an event that, when it is mentioned, you know what is being referred to – it's something in the environment.[20]

EL ANATSUI

In Africa, cloth may be used as a way of celebrating or commemorating something – an event, a particular person, a political cause – which in other parts of the world might be written down in detail and circumscribed with dates, or which might require a plaque or some other kind of monument. History in Africa may be read, told and recorded in cloth.

All artefacts or works of art conceived by the human mind hold within them stories which range far beyond the time of their creation or the lifetime of their creator, and African textiles are patterned with these hidden histories. From the two-million-year-old African hand-axes found at Olduvai Gorge in Tanzania to the sophisticated, multi-layered works produced by contemporary artists of African descent today, countless stories are locked up in these remarkable creations, though often we hear only one story, and even that may not spring from the work itself but from someone else's reaction to the work or to its creator. The history of Africa is often portrayed not as the living history of African people but as the history of the impact of other people upon African lives: the coming of the Phoenicians and Romans, the Arab invasions and the impact of Islam and Christianity, the Atlantic slave trade, the colonial period, the Cold War and so on. These histories are rarely told from an African perspective, let alone by an African voice. Museums often attempt to recreate the past through their collections in a linear, chronological fashion in which each object represents a particular moment in time. However, it is possible to portray the passage of time in a rather different way, as a cyclical phenomenon in which past, present and future are inextricably intertwined, as they often are in African oral history – and cloth provides a dynamic and fluid medium through which that history may be created and recorded.

Making and trading numerous types of cloth have been vital elements in African life and culture for at least two millennia, linking different parts of the continent with one another and with the rest of the world. Textile patterns, materials and means of production may illustrate individual events in history, or they may chart the movements and migrations of peoples over a much longer period; they may also tell of the long engagement of Africa with the Atlantic, Mediterranean and Indian Ocean worlds, charting the changes which have taken place in techniques, markets and materials, but also the continuity of ancient ideas and practices. Cloth may sometimes offer a means of understanding the religious, political, social or military history of African peoples in the absence of a detailed written historical account.

North and West Africa

The comparative fragility of textiles means that very few historical examples survive from sub-Saharan Africa, though recent archaeological research, notably at Kissi in Burkina Faso, suggests that woollen cloth was being used and traded in the region from at least the sixth century AD[21] and possibly earlier, though whether these textiles were being made locally or imported from North Africa is unclear. Wool and cotton fragments dating to the eleventh century AD discovered in four burial caves on the Bandiagara escarpment in Mali include narrow-strip weave and resist-dyed examples characteristic of sub-Saharan West Africa, as well as patterned cloth of North African inspiration.[22] Many centuries before the Portuguese navigated the West African coast in the fifteenth century, patterned textiles of essentially North African Amazigh (Berber) inspiration had been traded across the Sahara, then down the extensive waterways of the Niger, thus creating a taste for cloth of North African pattern among certain peoples of West Africa which remains to this day, despite the sumptuous textiles which they themselves produce. Similarly, the trade in the opposite direction may be reflected by some of the embroideries and woven cloth patterns of southern Tunisia and Libya, which show similarities to those of northern Nigeria and Cameroon.[23] However, as textile traditions developed to the north and south of the Sahara, it is difficult to pinpoint the original inspiration for certain contemporary practices.

Central Africa

In this kingdom of Congo they make some cloth of palm trees with a surface (skin) like velvet and some worked like velvety satin, so beautiful that those made in Italy do not surpass them in workmanship.[24]

D. PACHECO PEREIRA, *c*.1506

Even in the apparently remote regions of central Africa, textiles of great sophistication had been created from an early date using raffia palm fibre. As early as the sixteenth century, intricately patterned raffia cloth had been collected by Europeans from the estuary of the Congo River. Some of these cloths are included in the founding collection of the British Museum made by Sir Hans Sloane, though it was not until the display in the Museum of the collections made in the early twentieth century among the Kuba and other peoples of the Kasai/Kwilu region of the southern Congo Basin by Emil Torday, that their extraordinary artistry became more widely understood and appreciated.[25] Torday's collection had a profound effect on the British public and on artists of the time when it went on display at the British Museum in 1909. It was assumed that Kuba art, in common with the art of Benin in Nigeria, must have some distant connection with the Western tradition; except that here was a culture from the very heart of what was then often referred to as the 'Dark Continent'.

Eastern and southern Africa

The great cultures and empires of north-eastern and eastern Africa traded with Arabia, India and the Far East for at least a thousand years before Europeans arrived on the east coast of Africa in the late fifteenth century. The Swahili had established sophisticated stone towns along the coast, entrepôts for the equally sophisticated inland kingdoms including Ethiopia, Great Zimbabwe and Mapungubwe. Contemporary as well as historical textiles from the region reflect the development of this cultural complex. The great eighteenth-century wall hangings made for the Orthodox Christian Church in Ethiopia were created from Chinese silk, probably by Jewish weavers, and depict historical events, such as the funeral of King Bakaffa of Ethiopia (d. 1730), with such accuracy that we can tell that the firearms carried by some of his retinue depicted on the cloth are of Indian manufacture (see p. 41). It is hard to imagine a more cosmopolitan artefact.[26]

High-ranking Kuba-Ngongo woman wearing an appliqué raffia skirt. From a sketch made by Norman Hardy on Emil Torday's expedition in 1908, later worked up into a painting.

Today a bewildering array of printed textiles are worn or otherwise used in eastern and southern Africa, and most have hidden histories which may be read in their patterns and designs, or in their means of production. In its name alone the indigo blue patterned cloth *shweshwe* (see pp. 115–117) conjures the histories of many of the diverse peoples of southern Africa, and in particular the great Sotho leader King Moshoeshoe I (*c*.1786–1870) who was never defeated by Nguni, Boer or British forces, and to whom the modern, independent state of Lesotho owes its existence.

Two dance skirts with appliqué 'patches'
Raffia
Kuba-Ngongo people, Democratic Republic of Congo, 20th century
162 x 63 cm (right); 80 x 120 cm (below)
British Museum, Af1947,11.1 (right) and Af1969,02.2 (below), the latter
donated by Dennis Bullough

Long raffia textiles with appliqué 'patches' are created for use by women on ceremonial
occasions and are worn wound around the waist. Early examples (right) have few patches,
though more recently (below) the whole surface of the cloth is covered. The individual
motifs probably developed from the need to mend tears in plain cloth using patches, thus
creating an appealing pattern which was later replicated on cloths for aesthetic or symbolic
rather than practical reasons. Early dance skirts seem to include an outline of the famous
shongo or 'throwing-knife' (see below right) from which the Bushoong clan derive their
name: 'the people of the *shongo*/lightning'. Kuba oral history relates that the Bushoong
fought their way south to their present homeland using the throwing-knife, *shongo*, as their
primary weapon. In his book *On the Trail of the Bushongo*,[27] Emil Torday replicated an
image of the *shongo* which was drawn in the sand for him by the Kuba king (see opposite).
Torday believed that the ancient and extremely delicate and intricately patterned
embroidered raffia textiles of the Bushoong, the ruling clan of the Kuba, in some way
fulfilled the role of written manuscripts as a repository of Kuba history.

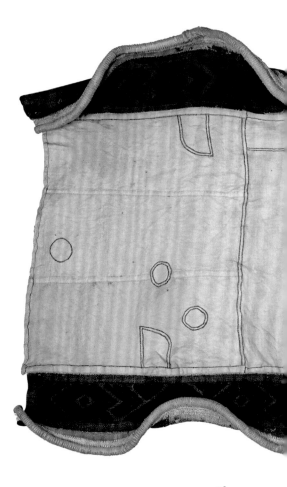

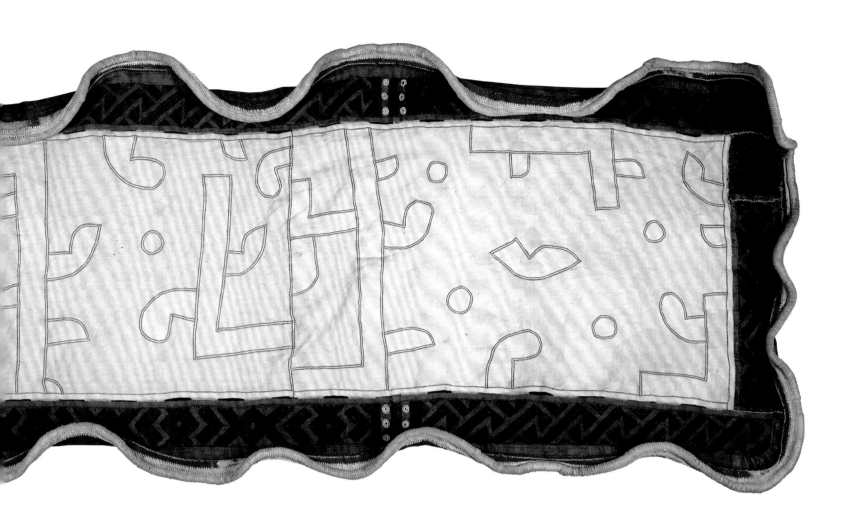

Shongo throwing-knife illustrated in Torday, E., 1925, *On the Trail of the Bushongo*, The Mayflower Press, Plymouth, p. 145. The weapon was no longer made or used by the Kuba when Torday conducted his research.

Cut-pile cloth
Raffia
Democratic Republic of Congo,
late 20th century
63 x 68 cm
British Museum, 2011,2029.1

The image of a leopard in this raffia cut-pile cloth may be a reference to the former dictator of Zaire, Mobutu Sese Seko, famous for his leopard-skin hats, pet leopards and other modern appropriations of ancient symbols of power.[28]

This late twentieth-century Bembe funerary figure from the Democratic Republic of Congo is clothed in at least four different types of leopard-skin print cloth. These small figures contain bones of deceased ancestors and are kept in the houses of important individuals where they are offered palm wine in exchange for ensuring continued good fortune. Private collection.

Printed Cloth

Cotton

Democratic Republic of Congo,
late 20th century

116 x 179 cm

British Museum, 2011,2002.24

This textile is printed with the names of various
Congolese newspapers. When Mobutu's dictatorship
finally came to an end in 1997, freedom of expression
and of the press was enshrined in articles 27 and 28 of
the transitional constitution of the Democratic Republic
of Congo (DRC). Despite ongoing violence and ethnic
conflict, freedom of the press is passionately defended in
DRC by organizations such as *Journaliste en Danger*
and is nationally and internationally recognized as vital
to a more settled and truly democratic future.

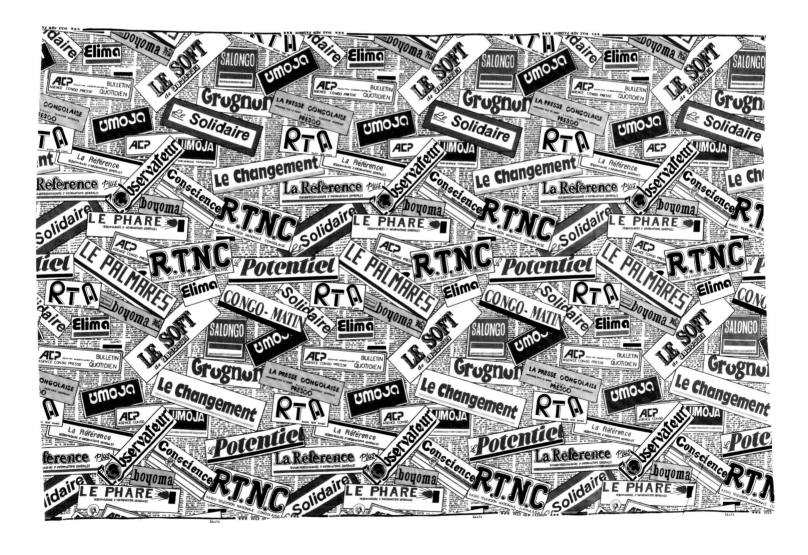

Honorific gown (*lemd*)
Silk, velvet, metallic thread
Ethiopia, mid 20th century
105 x 225 cm
British Museum, Af1974,11.11, donated by H. L. Littler

Prior to the Communist revolution of 1974, officers of church and state in Ethiopia wore honorific gowns, *lemd*, of silk and velvet, usually embellished with silver filigree work, as in this example which would have been worn on ceremonial occasions by a *Dejazmach* or general in the Ethiopian army. The silk would have been imported from China, while the silver wire would probably have been drawn from melted-down Maria Theresa 'dollars' or *thalers*. These silver coins were minted in Austria and traded in vast quantities to North and north-east Africa.

Tablet-woven church hanging (detail)
Silk
Gondar, Ethiopia, mid 18th century
306 x 63 cm
British Museum, Af1868,1001.22

This is the central panel of a tablet-woven triptych designed to screen the inner sanctum, *maqdas*, from the main body of an Ethiopian Orthodox Christian Church. It depicts in extraordinary detail the lying-in-state of King Bakaffa (pictured on p. 30), who died in 1730, and a funerary procession (as shown here) that includes his wife, Queen Mentuab and his seven-year-old son Iyasu, as well as angels and ecclesiastical and military figures. The cloth is made of imported Chinese silk, and the matchlocks carried by the royal guard (see below) are of Indian make, thus illustrating the long-standing trade and cultural exchange between eastern Africa and Asia. Tablet weaving in the region is associated with Jewish craftsmen, and it is possible that this triptych was commissioned from a specialist guild of Jewish weavers known to have been working across the Red Sea in the Yemen at this period.[29]

Patched garment (*muraqqa'a*)
Cotton, wool
North Sudan, late 19th century
91 x 159 cm
British Museum, Af1886,0628.1, donated by Surg-Maj H. J. Waller-Barrow

Muhammad Ahmad, the Mahdi or 'rightly guided one', led an uprising in late nineteenth-century Sudan which overthrew the Turkish-Egyptian government in Khartoum and established the Mahdist state. The first followers of the Mahdi wore patched, ragged tunics, *muraqqa'a*, to signal their contempt for worldly goods. The Mahdi died shortly after the fall of Khartoum in 1885 (AH 1302) and was succeeded by the Khalifa. In the ensuing years this ragged tunic was replaced by an altogether smarter garment, *jibba* (see opposite), which became the uniform of the Mahdists until the destruction of the state following the battle of Omdurman in 1898 (AH 1315). Once thought to have been the respective dress of rank and file and officer in the Mahdist armies, these two garments actually tell a much more subtle story which relates to the politics of costume and the evolution of the Mahdist state from a movement of religious zeal under the Mahdi to an increasingly militaristic autocracy under his successor, the Khalifa.[30]

Patched garment (*jibba*)
Cotton, wool
North Sudan, late 19th century
131 x 132 cm
British Museum, Af1980,01.1, donated by Mrs E. Pendlebury

The most common type of Mahdist tunic was particularly associated with the Baqqara (see p. 66), who rapidly became the ruling elite in the military autocracy which developed when their leader, the Khalifa, succeeded the Mahdi as ruler of Sudan in 1885 (AH 1302). However, Uthman Diqna, who was created Amir of the Beja peoples by the Mahdi in 1883 (AH 1300), was instrumental in encouraging the wearing of the *jibba* in this regional style calculated to unify the peoples of north-east Sudan in the Mahdist cause. The embroidery on the sleeves of this garment is similar to that which may be found on women's dresses among the Rashaida people of this region today.

Tunic with appliqué patches
Cotton, wool
Nigeria, late 20th century
133 x 168 cm
British Museum, 2008,2025.57

Tunics of this type refer to the patched garments (*jibba*) worn by the Mahdists in late nineteenth-century Sudan (see p. 43). Today such a garment might be worn on certain occasions by a Hausa chief or nobleman of northern Nigeria in place of his flowing, embroidered gown in order to emphasize his asceticism. Despite being a tailored, colourful version of the *jibba*, the patches on the garment retain their original significance as symbols of austerity and contempt for worldly goods.

Wall hanging (*drapeau*)
Cotton
Mali, mid 20th century
266 x 155 cm
British Museum, Af1990,12.5

This cotton wall hanging, or *drapeau*, was woven by a Fulbe weaver in Mali in the late 1970s and is a modern version of the classic woollen bed-screens (*arkilla kerka*, see p. 174) which formed an important part of a Fulbe bride's trousseau. This design known as 'General Soumare' was one of several created in the 1960s to celebrate the newly independent nation of Mali, emphasizing the green, gold and red colours of the Malian flag. The textile takes its name from the new passenger ship which sailed on the Niger between Koulikoro, Mopti and Gao, and in turn was named after General Abdoulaye Soumare (1905–64), a hero of the Malian independence struggle.[31]

Woman's ceremonial garment (*biskri*)
Cotton, silk, metallic thread
Djerba Island, Tunisia, 1998
389 x 147 cm
British Museum, Af1998,01.2

Master weaver Muhammed Tobji of
Djerba Island, Tunisia, with the woman's
ceremonial garment *biskri*.

The *biskri* is worn initially at marriage by women of Djerba Island, Tunisia. The pattern
bands have names such as 'beans', 'rice' and 'comb', which reflect concerns for fertility and
domestic harmony, as well as protection against the Evil Eye. This example was woven by
Muhammed Tobji of Djerba in 1998 (AH 1418). The name of the cloth is said to derive
from the town of Biskra in Algeria, though it is unclear whether Algerian weavers settled
on Djerba Island, or if the cloth was introduced, possibly via Libya, as a result of trade.[32]

Ceremonial tunic (*qmajja tawaliy*)
Cotton, silk
Mahdia, Tunisia, atelier of Karim
el-Arousse, 1998
133 x 116 cm
British Museum, Af1998,01.79

Young Tunisian girls from towns such as
Mahdia or Mokhnine may prepare twenty
to thirty of these ceremonial tunics, *qmajja
tawaliy*, for their trousseaux. The silk
ribbons (*hashiya*) which embellish this
garment are woven on a draw-loom in the
atelier of Karim el-Arousse, a master
weaver of Mahdia. The bride wears this
tunic for the seven days of the marriage
ceremony, while on the 'night of henna'
immediately before the ceremony she
dresses in seven tunics of graduating
length, one on top of another, as well as
having her hands, feet and face painted
with henna patterns to signify blessings,
fertility and protection from harm.
Straight, sleeveless tunics in similar form
were worn in this part of North Africa
when Carthage was at the height of its
power in the Greco-Roman world between
the seventh and second centuries BC.

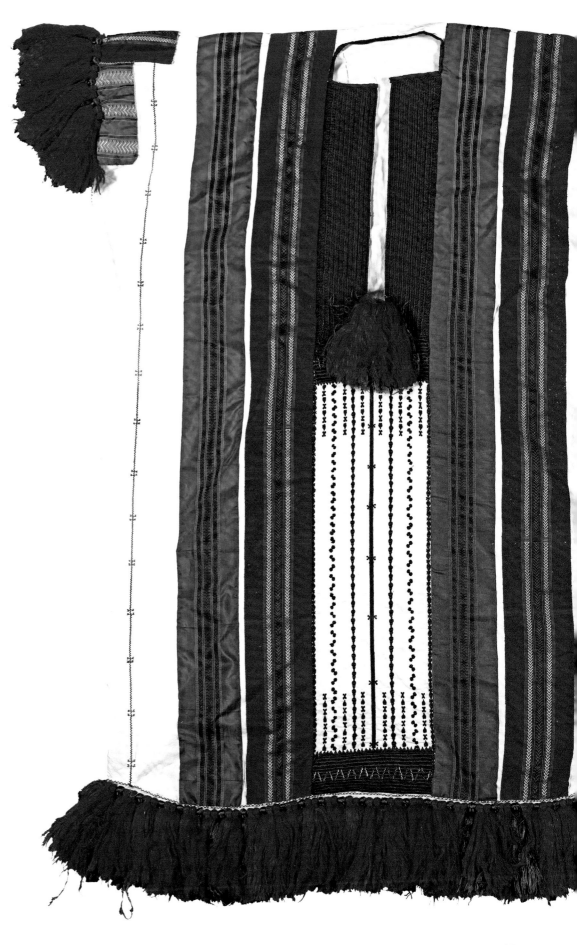

Narrow-strip cloth (*pano d'obra*)
Cotton
Manjak people, Guinea-Bissau, late 20th century
180 x 130 cm
British Museum, Af1989,05.164

This Manjak cloth displays the image of Amilcar Cabral, the revolutionary leader who led Guinea-Bissau to independence from Portugal in 1973. It represents a modern reflection of a historical process which has linked North Africa, the Iberian Peninsula and West Africa for more than a thousand years. The Manjak weavers of Guinea-Bissau and the hashiya weavers of Tunisia today use a 'draw-loom' which shares a common ancestor in the great draw-looms of the Hispano-Mauresque civilization that flourished in southern Spain, Portugal and North Africa from the tenth to the fifteenth centuries. Looms of this type are so named because they are fitted with a number of supplementary heddles that would be 'drawn up' by one or more assistants to the weaver. Today, Manjak weavers still use the looms and techniques which their ancestors learned from the Portuguese when brought as slaves to the Cape Verde islands in the sixteenth century.

Printed cloth (*capulana*)
Cotton
Mozambique, late 20th century
100 x 153 cm
British Museum, 2008,2012.4

This cloth commemorates the life of Josina Machel (1945–70), who was a key figure in the Mozambican independence struggle. She married Samora Machel, Mozambique's first president, and bore him a child, Samora Junior 'Samito', with whom she is pictured. Josina died at the age of twenty-five, though not before she had played a vital part in campaigning for the emancipation of women in Mozambique and in establishing a visionary social services programme. The Portuguese inscription on the textile translates as 'Josina Machel late lamented mother of the nation'.

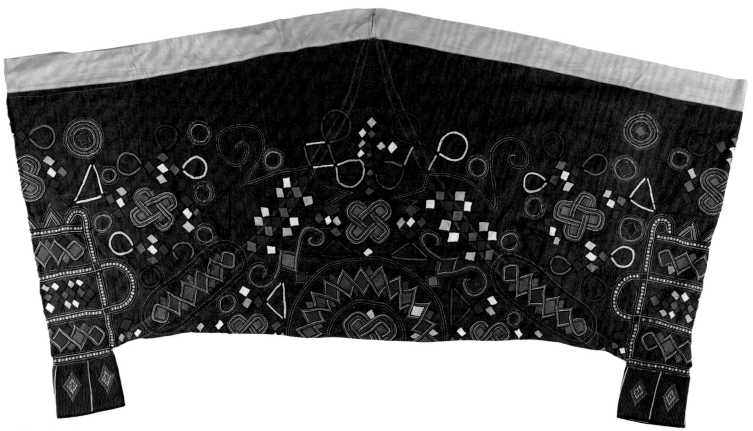

Embroidered trousers
Cotton, wool
Hausa people, Nigeria, 20th century
113 x 244 cm
British Museum, AOA 2008,2025.65

According to the Kano chronicle, a nineteenth-century document which draws together earlier manuscripts in tracing the history of this northern Nigerian emirate, the first Muslims came to Hausaland from Mali in the fourteenth century.[33] The great empires of the lands to the south of the Sahara all rose to prominence through the power of their horse-borne warriors, and a flowing gown and trousers with narrow leg openings (essentially riding breeches) became indicative of political and military power. The coming of Islam assimilated these and other traditions, closely associating these aspects of equestrianism and dress with the two major Muslim festivals of *'id al-fitr* and *'id al-kabir*. Interestingly, the style and colour of the embroidery on gowns – which was highly visible – and on trousers – which was covered by the gown and thus largely invisible – developed in very different directions. Embroidery on gowns, though often highly complex and elaborate, tends to be more monochrome and subdued, and its symbolism to be more concerned with protection from forces such as the Evil Eye. Embroidery on trousers, however, is more colourful and less restrained, and often includes a stylized version of the *agama* or 'rainbow' lizard, commonly associated with circumcision and male virility – two examples of this design run to left and right of the central motif on these trousers.[34] In both cases Islam has adopted and adapted much earlier traditions, and in this we can read much of the history of the religion as it has spread across North and West Africa.

Space Walk by Yinka Shonibare MBE, 2002
Screen printed cotton fabric, fibre glass, plywood, vinyl, plastic, steel

In his *Space Walk* the artist Yinka Shonibare MBE has created a male and female astronaut suspended from the ceiling alongside a space module named 'Martin Luther'. The astronauts – with their intricate oxygen packs and lifelines/umbilical cords connecting them to the mother ship – are dressed in Dutch 'wax' fabrics which are typical of Shonibare's work and which are popularly perceived as 'African' but in fact have a more complex cultural background. The fabrics for this installation were made by the artist in collaboration with the Philadelphia Fabric Workshop and represent an unique example of Shonibare designing his fabrics in response to a specific context. The spacesuits of the astronauts are embellished with images from album covers of famous R&B soul bands from the 'Philadelphia Sound' era. 'Philly Soul' was popularized in the 1960s by artists such as the Intruders, the Soul Survivors, the Delfonics and Patti LaBelle and appeared in the context of the nascent Civil Rights Movement and the accompanying black cultural explosion in the USA. Shonibare named the module 'Martin Luther' following the tradition of explorations made in the name of historical and political personalities. The choice of name, of course, also suggests Martin Luther King Jr, but simultaneously references a broader history of groundbreaking religious and civil figures.[35]

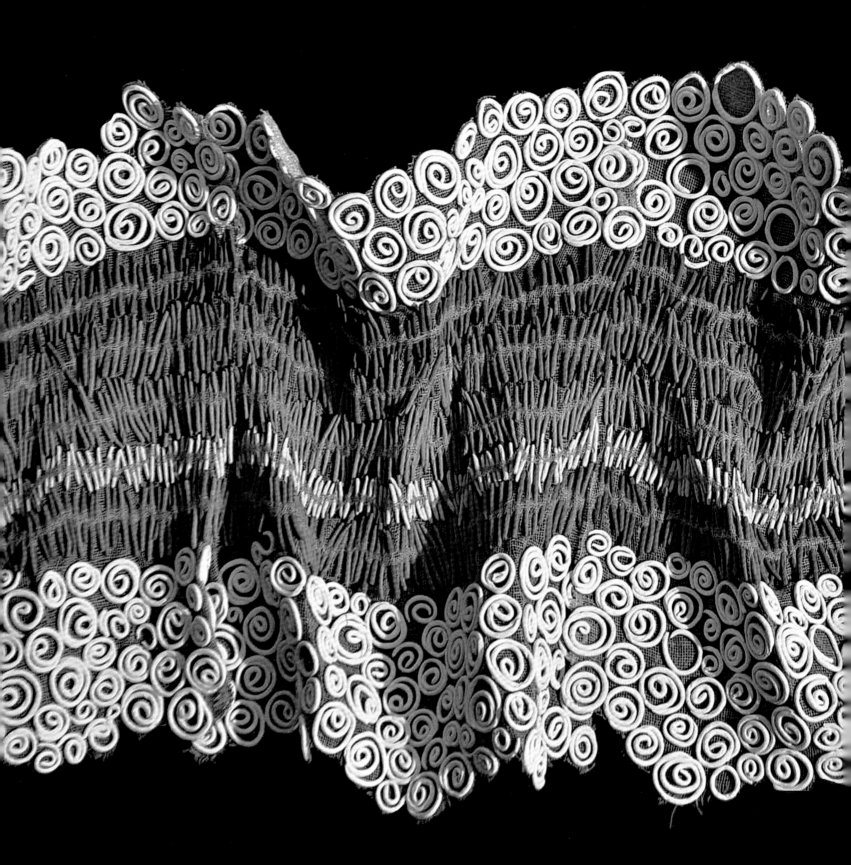

TEXTILES AND CONTEMPORARY AFRICAN ART

Agbogho (detail) by Nnenna Okore
Clay, burlap
Nigeria, 2009
122 x 213 x 15 cm

Okore studied sculpture under El Anatsui at the University of Nsukka in
Nigeria. In common with her mentor, many of her works relate to textile
forms on one level, but employ diverse materials such as fired clay to create
structure and patterning. 'I'm highly influenced by my Igbo homeland,' she
states, 'by its traditional and cultural processes, which have become a vivid
part of my make-up and memory'.[36] The title refers to the Igbo *Agbogho
Mmuo* or Maiden Spirit masquerade in which an elaborately decorated
knitted costume is worn by the masquerader, together with a white face
mask to suggest ideals of female beauty.

Textiles and contemporary African art

The history of indigenous African art has been misdirected by Western aesthetic preferences, which give an undue pride of place to figural or abstract sculpture (a pre-eminently patriarchal art) and less visibility to the role of textiles, decorative arts and performance arts (pre-eminently matriarchal arts) in the constitution of indigenous identity. The problem is that sculpture is actually a minor art in Africa … These important textiles ['wax' print, kente *and Kuba 'cut-pile'] have a universal recognition that African sculpture can only dream of. Anatsui's use of cloth as theme taps into this global awareness of its cultural power and efficacy as a deeply material and symbolic item of indigenous African culture.*[37]

SYLVESTER OKWUNODU OGBECHIE

Whether or not you agree with Ogbechie's assessment of the primacy of cloth among the arts of Africa, it is beyond question that many contemporary artists of African heritage have, one way or another, drawn inspiration from Africa's varied textile traditions. In 2008 two concurrent exhibitions in New York, one at the Metropolitan Museum of Art[38] and another at the Grey Art Gallery,[39] successfully highlighted this phenomenon, in the Met's case using the textile collections of the British Museum to make the point. Certain critics might have imagined that drawing inspiration from Africa's textile traditions could have made the work of the artists seem rather parochial, and that might have been the case if their work had merely been imitative of those traditions. In fact, what emerged from both shows was a feeling that the boundaries of what constitutes the field of artistic practice on a global stage had been expanded, because in each case the artists used textile traditions as means towards discussing ideas and concepts which have no national or even continental boundaries.

El Anatsui, in his vast, metal foil creations – which became internationally known through the touring exhibition *Gawu* organized by the Oriel Mostyn Gallery[40] – pursues a theme of transformation, which has pervaded much of his work by, as he says,'subverting the stereotype of metal as a stiff, rigid medium and rather showing it as a soft, pliable, almost sensuous material …'.[41] Created by many hands, these metal sculptures (see pp. 23 and 59) constantly change in shape and colour according to the different curators who install them. As shown in Chapter One (pp. 30–51), cloth is one of the main repositories of history in Africa and these works represent, among other things, the strength and beauty of African oral history, the unique qualities of which El Anatsui deeply respects. 'Oral histories', he observes, 'have the chance of being amended in the process of transfer through generations, without compromising their essential bases. It is easier to resolve varieties of the history and, in the process, history is edited by the owners of that history.'[42]

Although the narrow-strip *kente* cloth of his native Ghana is a pervasive presence, El Anatsui's technique of linking thousands of separate metal foil liquor bottle wrappers is totally different from the technique of weaving cloth and is now beginning to be acknowledged as a uniquely fluid medium of expression. As the curator and critic Robert Storr observed in the catalogue to the artist's 2010 exhibition organized by the Museum for African Art in New York,[43] 'Anatsui has engendered a fresh paradigm for abstraction and conjured a heretofore unanticipated – or more accurately, consistently overlooked – context in which that paradigm can and will flourish. His work is big news from Africa, but, even more important, it is world news for art.'

Atta Kwami, who, like El Anatsui, was born in Ghana, states of his working practice, 'I use oil on canvas, inks and acrylics on paper to portray a relationship between textiles, vision, time and the visual arts.'[44] (See p. 61.) He is impatient with the inadequacies of the critical criteria with which artists whose work has a superficial similarity (in Kwami's case a generalized notion of geometric abstraction) are compared and judged:

Although I find my work being compared with the work of other painters, surely that suggests only that several artists internationally are working in comparable ways? Yet my work is the outcome of a series of engagements with practices, forms and visual environments that are particularly specific to me in Ghana … all too often, opinion-makers from the West see their own art in innovative terms, while African art is inauthentic unless it can be seen to be rooted in tradition. Why not reverse the assessment and judge Western art by its authenticity and African art by its originality?[45]

If El Anatsui and Atta Kwami have used the leitmotif of *kente* cloth as means of beginning two different conversations with their audiences, Owusu-Ankomah, born in Ghana but now based in Germany, has done something similar with another textile tradition. His paintings depict a spiritual world, without light and shadow, occupied by people and by symbols which are used in the well-established Asante tradition of patterning cloth by means of *adinkra* designs cut into the surface of gourd hand-stamps. The way in which people and symbols co-exist in his paintings has moved through several distinct phases, which reflect Ankomah's own spiritual journey. Ankomah is profoundly influenced by the works of Michelangelo, 'this unbound energy, abounding with power, an exploding human adventure …',[46] and also by the philosophy of his own Akan-speaking peoples of Ghana, a philosophy which is reflected in their *adinkra* symbols, each of which represents a particular concept or proverb. Ankomah invests his figures with the almost divine energy of Michelangelo before painting their bodies with the collective wisdom of the Akan people in the form of *adinkra* symbols, to which he has added Chinese calligraphy, well-known popular logos and symbols of his own invention.

As a young man, El Anatsui had been influenced by a group of artists known as the Zaria Rebels, including the innovative printmaker Bruce Onobrakpeya, who had developed a movement called Natural Synthesis while studying in Zaria, Nigeria in the 1960s. This paved the way for Atta Kwami, Owusu-Ankomah and other artists to develop their practice in West Africa and around the world, often inspired and informed by textile traditions. At about the same time as the Zaria Rebels were making their mark in West Africa, the Khartoum School, under the leadership of Ibrahim El Salahi, began to be recognized in the 1960s as an emergent modernist movement producing a distinctive means of expression known as *Sudanawiyya* – a synthesis of Western styles of art with other traditions, reflecting the remarkable ethnic, religious and cultural diversity of Sudan, divided into two countries in 2011. Salahi explains part of the rationale behind the movement:

> *Originality, human originality, does not mean creating something out of nothing as such a claim is well beyond the capability of mankind. Originality in my opinion means to be able to create the new out of what is already there in existence. One simply makes a new addition, a sort of a new idea, a fresh leaf atop that same old tree of creation.*[47]

Among the traditions which inspire and inform Salahi's work is that of the patched and ragged garment, *muraqqa'a*, (see pp. 42 and 67) the wearing of which indicated a rejection of worldly goods by Sufi initiates in the Islamic world for centuries before the followers of the Mahdi in late nineteenth-century Sudan created, by his decree, their own version of this garment known as the *jibba* (see p. 43).

El Salahi helped to lay the groundwork for a generation of artists in North Africa, including Nja Mahdaoui in Tunisia (see p. 68), Rachid Koraïchi in Algeria (see p. 70), Ali Omar Ermes in Libya and Ahmed Moustafa in Egypt, who began to push the boundaries of acceptable practice in using calligraphy as an art form. Textiles, often in the form of giant hanging banners, offered a perfect base on which to explore some of these ideas, particularly in the work of Mahdaoui and Koraïchi. While always mindful of its sacred role of recording and revealing the word of God as set down in the holy Qur'an, these artists began to explore the artistic potential in the forms, rather than the literal meaning, of Arabic words and individual letters, and in the radically different types of script which had been developed by calligraphers over the centuries. Just as the textile traditions of West Africa had inspired El Anatsui and others, so the rich textile traditions of North and north-east Africa offered a variety of possibilities to artists from these regions.

Nja Mahdaoui experimented not only with his own personal 'calligrams' on conventional surfaces such as paper and parchment, but also embellished a range of other materials such as melamine, brass, aluminium and denim, as well as other forms including costume, musical instruments, buildings, the human body and even a jet aircraft.

Rachid Koraïchi also works with many media, including ceramics, textiles, poetry, calligraphy, light and paint. In common with El Salahi, he was born into an ancient Sufi brotherhood, and his work is intimately informed by the numerology, signs and ethos of Sufi mysticism and reflects the unique contribution of Africa to Islamic culture and philosophy. He has developed his own lexicon of signs and symbols based on Arabic, Amazigh (Berber), Chinese and Japanese characters and figures, as well as calligraphic motifs of his own invention and protective signs and symbols from North and West Africa, many of which are integral to the patterning of textiles.[48]

There is a long-standing myth that there are few indigenous textile traditions in eastern and southern Africa apart from on the island of Madagascar. As has already been suggested in this book, the idea of what constitutes an 'indigenous' tradition is, in any case, something which is very much open to debate. Around the world, particularly where different cultures meet, textiles have always reflected a diverse range of influences. The Indian Ocean coast of Africa has witnessed the arrival of traders and travellers from the east for at least two millennia, and for the past five hundred years from Europe and North America. In Chapter Four (pp. 98–119) we shall look at how the textile traditions of eastern and southern Africa have developed, but suffice it to say that artists from this part of the continent, including Peterson Kamwathi from Kenya, and Georgia Papageorge and Karel Nel from South Africa, have drawn inspiration from these traditions in different ways and, as elsewhere in Africa, have heightened the significance of textile traditions and of their own work by bringing them to a global stage.

Man's Cloth (detail) **by El Anatsui**
Metal foil
Nsukka, Nigeria, 2001
287 x 374 cm
British Museum, Af2002,10.1

Man's Cloth and *Woman's Cloth* (see p. 23) were the first works in which El Anatsui used foil liquor bottle wrappers, linked together in a technique which he described as part of the 'nomadic aesthetic': 'The nomadic aesthetic is about fluidity of ideas and impermanence of form, indeterminacy, as well as giving others the freedom, the authority to try their hands at forming what the artist has provided as a starting point'.[49] The brands of liquor used have names linked to events, people, historical or current issues. Traditional silk *kente* cloths are also named in this way. History in Africa may be read in cloth. Despite the beauty of this transformation of liquor bottle wrappers, the grim realities of the Middle Passage, in which liquor was one of the primary commodities exchanged for enslaved Africans, is also never far away.

Narrow-strip cloth (*kente*)
Silk
Asante people, Ghana, mid 20th century
300 x 190 cm
British Museum, Af1947,06.2

The production, use and distribution of complex patterned silk textiles such as this (commonly known as *kente* outside Asante) became one of the most prestigious symbols of leadership at the Asante court in Kumase, Ghana. Today, the finest of these textiles are still made near to the capital city in the village of Bonwire by specialist weavers. Certain silk cloths, notable for their complex weft inlay patterns entirely covering the warp (*asasia*), were reserved for the *Asantehene* (king) and his immediate family. The name of the overall design is derived from the warp striping. Many of the names are descriptive and refer to famous rulers or individuals, while others are associated with special events. Narrow-strip woven silk cloth was once a monopoly of the *Asantehene* and royal lineage of the Asante of Ghana. Today *kente* cloth is widely worn, but remains a symbol of African independence and culture throughout the world.

Kokrobite by Atta Kwami
Acrylic on canvas
Kumase, Ghana, 2007
147 x 165 cm
British Museum, 2010,2003.1

Speaking of works such as *Kokrobite* the artist Atta Kwami states, 'The starting point of my inspiration is my environment. Many of my images have been shaped by my experiences of Atonsu Agogo, a commercial/workshop area in Kumase close to my studio.' One of Atta Kwami's earliest memories is of the tablets of brilliantly coloured paint in his mother Grace Kwami's studio. Two other aesthetic and intellectual influences from the rich visual environment of Kumase have had a profound effect on him: the textile tradition and the art of commercial sign painters. 'I have focused on colour as subject matter, perhaps taking me back to what I started with as a child, in my mother's studio; the perception of colour-tablets in tins. My mother's paints and her textiles were a good resource.' 'Kokrobite' is the name of a small coastal village about an hour from Accra; the Kokrobite Institute offers a retreat for students to come and learn about Ghanaian and African culture.[50]

Atta Kwami's work, including monumental hangings and three-dimensional structures, at the third Sansa workshop, National Cultural Centre, Kumase, 2009, supported by the Triangle Arts Trust and the British Museum's Africa Programme.

***Adinkra* cloth (detail)**
Cotton, silk
Ghana, early 21st century
109 x 125 cm
British Museum, Af2006,15.181

Adinkra cloth with strips of woven *kente*
cloth dividing the squares containing
stamped symbols, which include the
adinkrahene symbol of concentric circles,
the *akoben* or war horn, a crescent on top
of three triangles, meaning vigilance and
caution, and *funtunfunefu* or linked
crocodiles representing democracy.

Free (detail) by Owusu-Ankomah
Acrylic on canvas
Bremen, Germany, 2007
150 x 200 cm
British Museum, 2012,2012.1

In his painting *Free*, one of a series to mark the bicentenary of the Abolition of the Atlantic slave trade, Owusu-Ankomah uses traditional symbols of *adinkra* cloth as well as of his own creation. The concentric circles on the chest of the central figure are the *adinkrahene*, the chief of all the *adinkra* symbols, which represents greatness, charisma and leadership. Owusu-Ankomah describes this symbol as '... an emanation from his inmost being which cries out "I am open, talk to me! My heart is receptive, I am full of love!" To me this is the message which most needs to be spread around these days, for with it we can change the world'. The artist goes on to say, 'The figure in *Free* is caught in a moment of transcendence. Close observation might remind the viewer of two monumental sculptures, one found on each of the American continents: the Statue of Liberty in New York, and that of Christ the Redeemer in Rio de Janeiro.'[51]

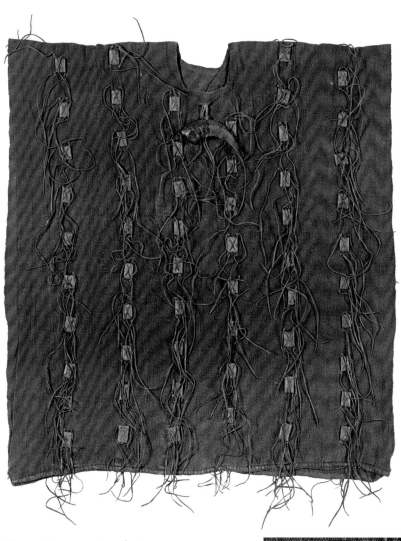

Protective gown (*ronko*)
Cotton, leather
Mende people, Sierra Leone,
early 20th century
95 x 88 cm
British Museum, Af1904,0415.21

Hunter or soldier's protective gown from
Sierra Leone with numerous charms
(*gris-gris*) in the form of small leather
packages attached. These packages might
contain magical or protective devices such
as quotations from the Qur'an or objects
to ward off the Evil Eye.

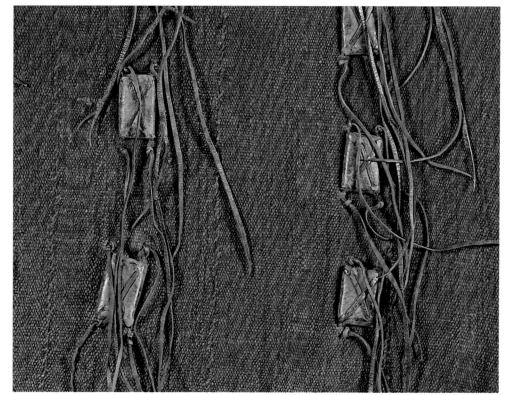

Pouvoir et Religion (Power and Religion) by Abdoulaye Konaté, 2011, commissioned by INIVA (Institute of International Visual Arts)

Abdoulaye Konaté has a deep knowledge of and admiration for the way of life of the Mandé hunters of Mali. In common with many of the peoples living in the Sahel region to the south of the Sahara, Mandé hunters wear tunics covered with charms or *gris-gris* to protect them from harm. These charms can take many forms though usually the object of power and protection is wrapped or contained in some way. In this work Konaté uses layered strips of cloth to suggest these charms, in stylized form, as well as the plumage of the guinea fowl. The artist questions the ambiguous position which heads of government take towards religion. The ambiguity is best expressed by the Malian writer Massa Malandiabaté: 'The guinea fowl spreads out its colours over its plumage – and man keeps them in his heart.'

Below The commissioned work in the gallery of INIVA, London, 2011, and close-up detail shown *right*.

Patched tunic (*jibba*)
Cotton, wool
Baqqara people, North Sudan, late 19th century
90 x 125 cm
British Museum, Af1972,11.14, donated by Miss M. Collins

The patched tunic, *jibba*, was the distinctive uniform of the followers of Muhammad
Ahmad, the Mahdi or 'rightly guided one' who in 1884 (AH 1301) led a *jihad* or Holy War
to establish the Mahdist State in Sudan. The *jibba* was inspired by the ragged *muraqqa'a*
(see p. 42) which for centuries had been the dress of the Sufi religious orders, signifying their
contempt for worldly goods. There were different regional styles of *jibba* – this example is
typical of those worn by the Baqqara of Kordofan and is quite different in size, colour and
design from those worn by, for example, the Beja of north-eastern Sudan (see p. 43).

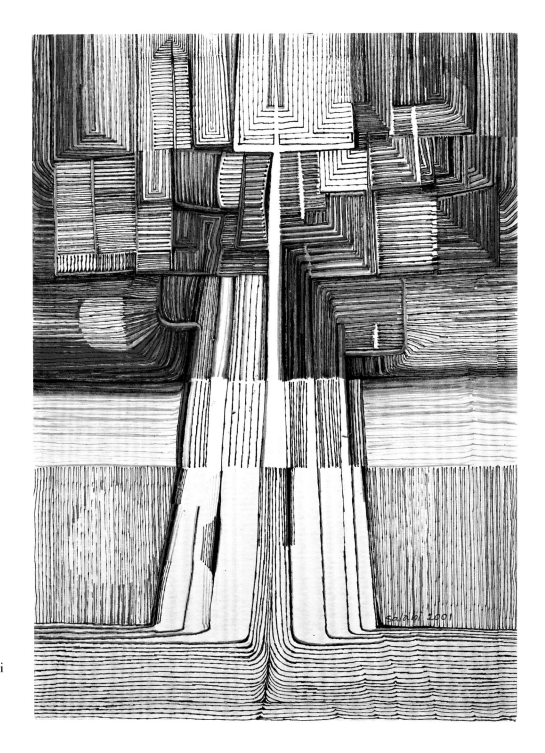

From the *Tree* series by Ibrahim El Salahi
Coloured inks on paper
Oxford, UK, 2001 (AH 1421)
35 x 26 cm
British Museum, 2010,2037.1

The artist Ibrahim El Salahi, himself a member of a Sufi brotherhood, sees the *jibba* as a metaphor for the remarkably diverse nature of Sudanese society, the patches symbolizing different cultures and beliefs in various parts of the country. In this work from the *Tree* series (2001/AH 1421) El Salahi makes reference to the form of the *jibba* as well as to the human form, suggesting a Tree of Life in Sudan. Although the Mahdist State ceased to exist following the Battle of Omdurman in 1898 (AH 1315), Mahdism, through the mouthpiece of the Umma party, remains a vital political force in North Sudan today.

Bandiera (detail) by Nja Mahdaoui
Discharge-dyed denim
Tunisia, 1997 (AH 1417)
149 x 632 cm
British Museum, Af1998,03.2

This wall hanging was created on high quality denim, normally used for making designer jeans, by the Tunisian artist Nja Mahdaoui and is similar to those used as a backdrop to his monumental musical and visual installation at Tunis railway station (see opposite) celebrating the end of Ramadan in 1997 (AH 1417). Mahdaoui is not concerned with the meaning of words ('words restrict meaning,'[52] he observes) but rather to transform them into 'calligrams' of his own invention, here applied with loose strokes of a brush loaded with a caustic solution which 'discharges' the dye from the denim. By this means he releases their potential, in combination with colour, to evoke a range of sensations, from intense visual pleasure, to the melodies and rhythms of music and the collective passion of religious devotion.

Tunis railway station with Mahdaoui's banners in the distance, celebrating *'id al-fitr*, the end of Ramadan, 1997 (AH 1417). A large decorated drum (now British Museum, Af1998,03.1) is at the front of the stage.

Untitled banner by Rachid Koraïchi
Black acrylic on silk
Algeria, 1989 (AH 1409)
310 x 195 cm
British Museum, Af1997,08.2

This silk banner by the Algerian-born artist Rachid Koraïchi incorporates a range of magical and protective signs and symbols, prevalent across North and Islamic West Africa, which he places alongside letters and numbers from Arabic and the Tamazight (Berber) script. Koraïchi was born into a Sufi family in Algeria; he frequently produces works in a series of seven or uses seven elements in his designs, which refer to the Muslim cosmogony of seven heavens, seven planets and seven periods of creation. In amongst these Koraïchi inserts cryptograms of his own inspiration. He collaborates closely with local weavers, embroiderers and other artists to create his works. The silk cloth onto which Koraïchi applied his calligraphy was woven in Tunisia, a country still famous for its silk weavers. The banner emphasizes the cultural diversity of North Africa and Islamic West Africa, but also suggests a common magical and symbolic language which pervades the region.

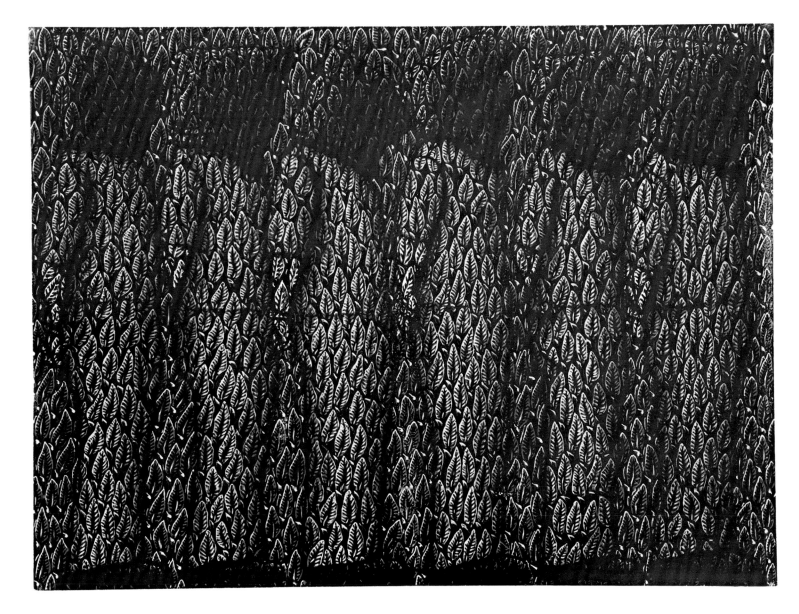

Untitled woodcut print on paper from the
Queue **series by Peterson Kamwathi**
Kenya, 2010
89 x 122 cm
British Museum, 2012,2010.1

In his series of untitled woodcut prints, the Kenyan artist Peterson Kamwathi uses the striking image of people queuing, creating echoes of the published images of blindfolded prisoners from Afghanistan or hooded prisoners from Guantanamo Bay.[53] Kamwathi makes these images all the more poignant by covering the figures in the repeating patterns of flowers and leaves seen on the printed cloths of the region, *kanga* and *kitenge*. In eastern Africa, as in other parts of Africa, women (in particular) and men may dress in the same pattern and colour of cloth to show unity and friendship, whether at a wedding, a funeral or some other special event.

Nine Flags by Raimi Gbadamosi
Cotton, copper
London, UK, 2000
210 x 100 cm each
British Museum, 2011,2038.1.a–i

Nine Flags is a conceptual work which extends our notions of Britishness and British-associated identities in offering a decolonization of the Union Jack (see below for key to the different flags). One interpretation of the central flag of the 'nine' is that it suggests an idea of Africa by taking the colours (black, red and green) of Marcus Garvey's pan-African banner, and at the same time mocking the old British National Front slogan, 'There ain't no black in the Union Jack'. The central position of this flag also suggests the centrality of Africa in the history of human life on earth and its identity as the place where the most ancient examples of 'artistry' were created, evoking an Africa which is both a continent of that name and a phenomenon that reaches out to every corner of the globe.[54]

Key to the flags
Each of the flags represents not an individual nation state, but a loose grouping of peoples defined sometimes by ethnicities, sometimes by geographical location, occasionally by both:

Top row (from left to right): the Arab World; southern Europe; Korea, Japan and South East Asia
Middle row (from left to right): China and India; Africa; the Celtic nations.
Lower row (from left to right): the Anglo Diaspora, including Australia, Canada and the USA; the Caribbean and South America; Scandinavia.

***The Long March of Displacement* by Leo Asemota, 2009**

Leo Asemota (left) and two assistants pose in front of the Houses of Parliament, London, as the 'Agents of the Union' in his work *The Long March of Displacement*, set on the arc of the Victoria Embankment from Westminster Bridge to Blackfriars Bridge en route to St. Paul's Cathedral. The performance was informed by two events with correlating timelines: 1897, the year of Queen Victoria's Diamond Jubilee (commemorated by an inscription in the pavement outside St. Paul's) and also the year of the British capture and looting of Benin City. The 'uniforms' worn by the Agents were carefully chosen by Asemota to suggest not only the uniforms of the African colonial troops of the Gold Coast Protectorate (now Ghana) who took part in the operation and in the capture of the Oba (king) of Benin, but also elements of Benin royal regalia, in particular the Oba's ceremonial garments. These garments were made of red coral, which are reflected in the coral caps worn by the Agents, caps which today are worn by wealthy Nigerian men on important occasions. Around their waists they wear woven sashes of black and silver lurex cloth, and on their feet webbed 'foot-gloves' of the type worn for kayaking and other water sports, underlining the Oba's dominion over land and sea.[55]

FABRIC OF A NATION: PRINTED CLOTH OF WEST AFRICA

Seated beneath his ceremonial umbrella (*ahenfo kyeniwa*), the *Asonahene* of Akim Osorase (Chief Nana Nyarko Ababio) is robed in hand-woven *kente* cloth, strips of which are incorporated in the white robe of the Queen Mother of Akim Kebi who is seated on his right. The woman presenting him with cloth is the celebrator of the chief, and is robed in a 'fancy' print version of *kente*. The bowl of cloth, which she has carried before him in procession, represents the chief's wealth, while the gold-hilted sword represents his power and status. The chief's linguists, *akyeame*, stand behind him and act as his spokesmen or 'interpreters' on ceremonial occasions. The Queen Mother's 'linguist' sits on the left of the chief and wears a skirt which displays a modern variation of the 'flying ducks' design (see p. 81). Chief Ababio works at the British Museum.

Fabric of a nation: printed cloth of West Africa

The fabrics are not really authentically African the way people think; they prove to have a crossbred cultural background quite of their own. And it's the fallacy of that signification that I like.[56]

YINKA SHONIBARE MBE

In 2007 the British Museum opened an exhibition entitled *Fabric of a Nation: Textiles and Identity in Modern Ghana*[57] at the same time as a 'sister' exhibition opened at the Department of Archaeology at the University of Ghana at Legon.[58] The exhibitions were initially intended to celebrate the fiftieth anniversary of Ghana's independence on 6 March 2007, but several years later the British Museum's highly successful exhibition was still touring to venues in the UK.

Although the titles of these exhibitions did not specify which of Ghana's many textile traditions they took as their subject, they did in fact concentrate on the factory-made 'wax' and 'fancy' prints, collectively known as 'Mammy Cloth',[59] which imitate Javanese batik resist-dyed cloths. (The name 'Mammy Cloth' may derive from the first commemorative portrait reproduced on cloth for the West African trade in 1928. It depicts a woman, perhaps a market trader, and was simply entitled 'Mammy'.) This chapter expands on some of the themes of those pioneering exhibitions and broadens their scope to include the whole of West Africa, where these textiles have been popular for almost two centuries. However, the story begins in Ghana, where not only was the taste for factory-printed cloth first acquired, but also a well-established system of hand-stamping cloth with *adinkra* symbols had developed among the Asante people. It was, therefore, not surprising that *adinkra* symbols and other motifs suggestive of well-known proverbs were included in the earliest designs created in Europe for sale to West Africa on factory-printed cloth patterned in imitation of Javanese batiks. The complex history of these cloths links the continents of

Adinkra stall, with carved *adinkra* stamps in the foreground. Ntonso, Asante region, Ghana, 2010.

Asia, Africa and Europe in a fascinating sequence of events.[60]

The Dutch textile industry had suffered because of the Napoleonic Wars at the beginning of the nineteenth century. One possible means of reviving this industry seemed to be offered by the Dutch colonization of Indonesia and by the production of a mechanized version of hitherto labour-intensive, hand-stamped Javanese batiks. Unfortunately, the mechanically produced imitations were not a hit with the Javanese, though it seems that they did appeal to mercenary soldiers from Ghana (in those days known as the Gold Coast) whom the Dutch had employed to police their new colonies in Indonesia. When these soldiers returned home they brought with them cloths that included the characteristic 'crackling' effect, caused by faults in the manufacturing process, which had proved so unappealing to the Indonesians.

It did not take long for the Dutch and British to realize that what had been a failure in Indonesia could be a commercial success in Africa, but for it to be so it had to be driven by African taste, aesthetics and patronage. The early designs of these cloths, therefore, visualized concerns such as those expressed through local African proverbs, as well as subjects such as kingship, education and resistance to colonial rule. From the 1850s the Dutch firm of van Vlissingen & Co (today still operating as Vlisco) began exporting printed cloth to West Africa. In 1893, while working as an agent for the Dutch Haarlem Cotton Company, the Scottish trader Ebenezer Brown Fleming set up his own firm in Glasgow and pirated Dutch designs for trade to West Africa. The earliest recorded and confirmed date for one of these cloths, 1895, was identified by John Picton[61] in the archive of the Manchester-based factory ABC (Arthur Brunnschweiler & Company). That 1895 cloth bears a design which is still printed today, incorporating fingers, coins and a hand – a Ghanaian proverb which broadly means that 'if you go it alone you will fail, but if you work together you can make money'. It also refers to the Akan proverb, 'The palm of the hand [that is, where money is received] is sweeter than the back of the hand' (see p. 120).

Technical innovations in the mechanical production of these cloths included the invention of duplex rollers, which allowed the application of a resin resist agent to both sides of the cloth, a process undertaken by hand in Javanese batiks. Then in the 1920s a process was invented which did not require a resist agent at all and allowed printing on one side of the cloth only, while at the same time reproducing some of the features of 'wax' prints. These cloths became known as 'fancy' prints. They were not only cheaper than 'wax' prints, but allowed for the reproduction of photographic images for the first time. This in turn led to a rapid development in the tradition of commemorative cloths in which people and important events could be celebrated. In the post-colonial period the production of 'wax' and, in particular, of 'fancy' prints represented not only an opportunity to celebrate particular individuals, but also became an increasingly important political tool, as well as promoting businesses, religious beliefs, schools, universities, and awareness of health issues.

This led to the establishment of textile factories in various West African countries, including Sotiba in Senegal, Afprints in Nigeria, Uniwax in Ivory Coast and GTMC in Ghana. These companies became important producers of textiles not just for the African market but also, in Sotiba's case in particular, the leading producer of 'African print' fabrics in the USA.[62] In recent years, African production of 'wax' and 'fancy' prints has been seriously threatened by cheap Chinese textiles imitating many of the most popular West African designs. Copyright protection of these designs by African governments is a hard case to argue when so many cultures and so many companies in different parts of the world have been involved in their production for so long. One thing is certain – African patronage and African taste will continue to drive the trade as it always has done, whoever produces the cloth.

Creating *adinkra* cloth using silk screen printing. Ntonso village, Asante region, Ghana 2010.

Hand-stamped *adinkra* cloth (detail)
Cotton
Asante people, Ghana, early 20th century
232 x 112 cm
British Museum, Af1935,1005.2, donated by A. F. Kerr

The earliest *adinkra* cloth in the British Museum's collection was acquired by T. E. Bowdich in 1817, but as mentioned in the introduction, *adinkra* symbols have been in use for many centuries, though it is not known when they began to be applied to cloth. The motifs are applied to cotton base cloth using stamps cut from pieces of gourd. The dye used is prepared from bark of the *badie* tree, boiled up with lumps of iron slag to produce a black, viscous liquid. In common with the woven textiles of the Asante, each *adinkra* cloth and each individual motif is given a name, which may have a magical, historical or proverbial significance. Cloths dyed blue (such as this example) or red are worn at funerals, whereas those that retain a white background are worn on other important occasions.

Wax-printed cloth with 'flying ducks' design (detail)
Cotton
Manchester, UK, early 20th century
93 x 90 cm
British Museum, Af 1934,0307.414, donated by Charles A. Beving

One of the very early designs created in the nineteenth century for the West African trade
was known as 'flying ducks', although their long, narrow bills and short wings suggest
that the original designer probably had some other birds, such as snipe, in mind. The
design remains extremely popular today. The bird is a symbol of good fortune and the
family of birds depicted on this textile suggest shared and long lasting happiness.

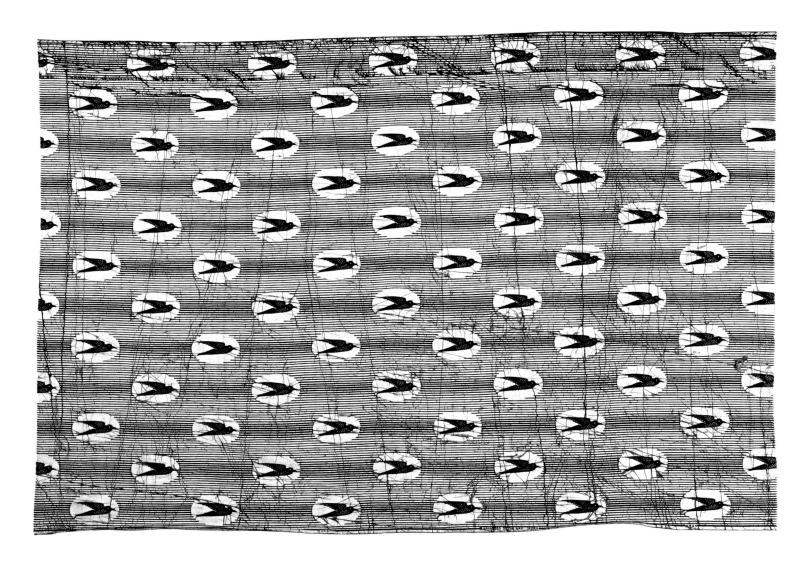

**Wax-printed cloth with
'Speed bird' design**
Cotton
Netherlands/West Africa, 1980s
114 x 179 cm
British Museum, 2011,2002.41

In common with 'flying ducks', 'Speed
bird' is one of the early designs of wax-
printed cloth which has remained popular.
John Picton[63] advised me that in Ghana
this design acquired the name *Sika wo
ntaban*, 'Money has wings', in other words
you never know when good fortune will
come or go. The design is worn in many
parts of West Africa, though colour
preferences vary.

Still Life: Lying Down Textiles by Grace Ndiritu
UK, 2005–7

The artist Grace Ndiritu often uses cloth in her work. This image is taken from one of
the four 'video paintings' which make up the work *Still Life*. In *Lying Down Textiles* she
portrays herself wrapped in printed cloth with the 'speed bird' design prominent in the
backdrop – for an artist, the idea that 'money has wings' is an all too familiar concept.
This yellow version of the design is popular in Mali, where Ndiritu obtained the cloth,
though in Ghana and Nigeria blue or black is the preferred colour.

Wax-printed cloth (detail)
Cotton
Agona Swedru, Ghana, early 21st century
119 x 506 cm
British Museum, Af2006,15.9

The design of this cloth is based on the
proverb, 'Your eyes can see, but your mouth
cannot say'; in other words, some issues
should not be discussed in public even though
you can see the problem quite plainly.

Stencilled *adire eleko* cloth (detail)
Indigo resist-dyed cotton
Yoruba people, Abeokuta, Nigeria, late 20th century
179 x 162 cm
British Museum, Af1971,35.26

The word *adire* in Yoruba means 'to tie and dye'; to this are added words describing the various techniques of 'tie and dye', such as *adire oniko* (raffia tied) or *adire alabere* (raffia stitched). The overall designs of *adire* cloths are also named. If starch paste (*eleko*) is used as the resisting agent, the cloth is known as *adire eleko*. The town of Abeokuta was known for using stencils to apply the starch paste, as in this example, whereas the designs were largely hand painted in Ibadan. The words OGUN PARI mean 'war has finished' in Yoruba, and refer to the end of the Nigerian Civil War. Although the official ceasefire came in January 1970, the date '4.10.70' commemorates the announcement by General Gowon of the nine tasks to be achieved before handing over to a civilian government. The image of the king derives from an earlier cloth commemorating the installation of the new *Alake* (king) of Abeokuta in 1963. Both cloths have a common origin in the *adire* cloths that use an image of King George V and Queen Mary, which appeared on various souvenirs to commemorate the King's Silver Jubilee in 1935.

Wax-printed cloth with Ananse design
Cotton
Netherlands/Ghana, 1992
115 x 181 cm
British Museum, 2011,2002.73

Ananse the spider is a joker, a trickster and a folk hero whose stories and wisdom have spread to many parts of the world beyond his home in Ghana.[64] The Atlantic slave trade ensured that Ananse in his various guises is part of the fabric of life in the Caribbean and the southern USA.

Commemorative cloth (detail)
Cotton velvet
UK/Nigeria, 1939
187 x 112 cm
British Museum, 2009,2020.1, donated
by Mrs Leah Williams

Cotton sheeting is by far the most versatile
base material for all types of hand- and
factory-printed cloth, but occasionally
other materials, such as velvet, were used
in West Africa. This early commemorative
cloth had been in the family of Mrs Leah
Williams for many years and probably
celebrates the life of Mary Jibowu, the
mother of Sir Olumuyiwa Jibowu (1899–
1959), the first African to serve on the
Supreme Court of Nigeria during the
colonial period.

Fancy-printed cloth

Cotton

Central African Republic, 1999

118 x 182 cm

British Museum, 2011,2002.2

Mireille Kolingba is the wife of André Kolingba, president of the Central African Republic from 1981–93. This cloth was produced after her husband had left office and celebrates her role as honorary president of the *Union Démocratique des Femmes Centrafriques*. The Women's Union and other women's organizations are extremely important in African societies and are seen as cohesive forces and guardians of culture and education. Interestingly, Mireille Kolingba's own political career blossomed long after her husband's had ended when she was elected an MP in 2005.

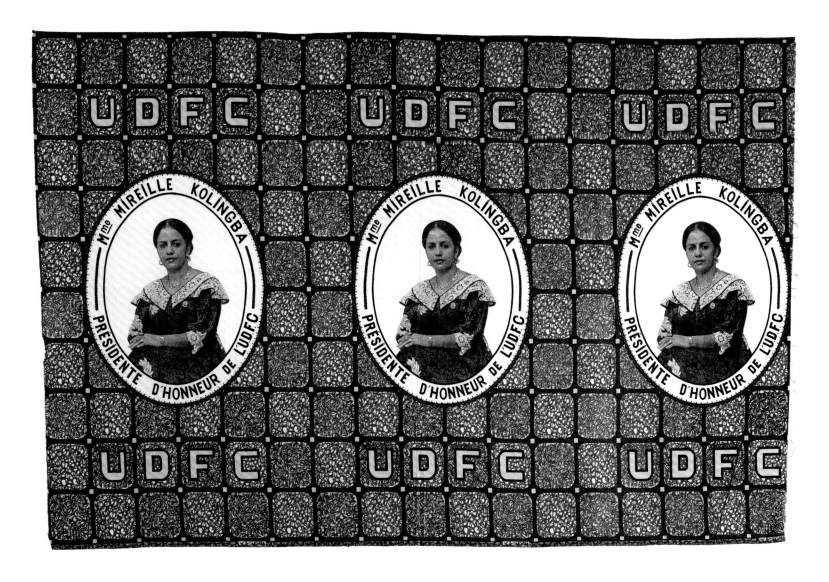

**Untitled performance
by Akwele Suma Glory**
Lagos, Nigeria, 2010

This work was performed by the Ghanaian artist Akwele Suma Glory at the Stone House artists' workshop, Lagos, Nigeria in 2010. The workshop was supported by the Centre for Contemporary Arts, Lagos, the Triangle Arts Trust and the British Museum's Africa Programme. The artist describes the work as follows:

In this particular body of work, my untitled performance (Transformational Change) brings into dialogue two specific textile forms that exist in Ghana, Kente and wax print. I am adorned in wax print and a wig, standing against a wall onto which I have pasted newspaper cuttings, gleaned from the Nigerian press. I slowly shed off the kente *cloth, and pull off the wig to expose my natural hair, I then walk slowly off. These actions speak to the general ambivalent state of independence in such sub-Saharan countries as Ghana and Nigeria. The rather short performance (approximately three minutes) also questions claims to authenticity (represented by the* kente *cloth and my natural hair) and what can be read as un-authenticity (fakeness) signified by the wax print, manufactured in 'China' and the un-natural hair (wig).*[65]

Fancy-printed cloth
Cotton
UK/Ghana, 1957
121 x 193 cm
British Museum, Af1993,15.2, donated
by Mr E. D. Captan

On 6 March 1957 Ghana became one
of the first African countries to gain
independence from colonial rule, an event
commemorated on this 'fancy' print,
together with the country's first Prime
Minister Dr Kwame Nkrumah (1952–66).
In his opening address to the nation he
stated, 'Our independence is meaningless
unless it is linked up with the total
liberation of the African continent'.[66]

**Fancy-printed dress with images of
President Obama and President Mills**
Cotton
China/Ghana, 2009
133 x 131 cm
British Museum, 2011,2001.1, donated
by Elsbeth Court

Ghana was delighted (and Kenya slightly
annoyed) that Barack Obama chose the
former country for his first state visit to
sub-Saharan Africa following his election as
US President in 2009. 'Africa doesn't need
strong men, it needs strong institutions,'
said President Obama, addressing the
Ghanaian parliament. This dress, showing
images of President and Mrs Mills of
Ghana as well as of Barack and Michelle
Obama, was tailored from 'fancy' print
fabric manufactured in China.

Portrait by Jacques Touselle
Photo
Mbouda, Cameroon, 1977

Coronations, as well as royal and state
visits, were frequent subjects for
commemorative cloths from the 1930s
onwards. The Cameroonian photographer
Jacques Touselle[67] took this portrait in his
studio in Mbouda, a small provincial town.
The woman in this photograph wears a
printed ensemble celebrating the Silver
Jubilee of Queen Elizabeth II in 1977.

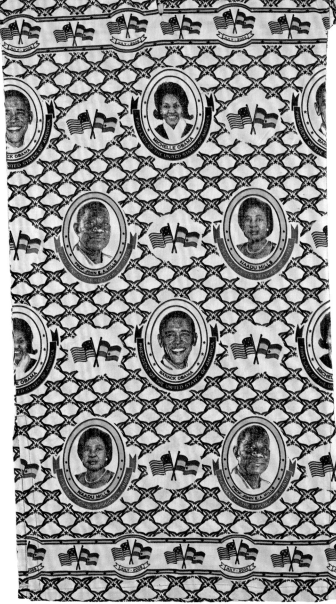

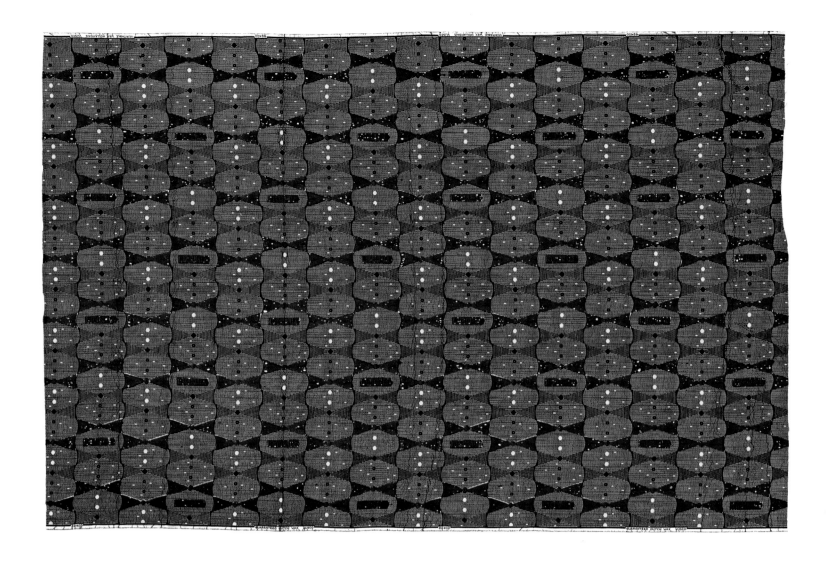

Wax-printed cloth, 'HIGH-LIFE'
Cotton
Netherlands/Ghana, late 20th century
118 x 182 cm
British Museum, 2011,2002.77

Important politicians and other celebrities are not the only subjects of commemorative
cloths. Sometimes sporting or cultural achievements are celebrated, including the musical
phenomenon known as 'High-life', a fusion of Western and African musical styles which is
still popular today, but which had its heyday in Ghana and Nigeria in the decades following
the Second World War. There are different styles of High-life, each with its own legendary
performers, such as E. T. Mensah with his Big Band sound, and E. K. Nyame with his
'rural' guitar-based band. In the late 1960s and early 70s bands such as Osibisa brought a
rock version of High-life to Europe and the USA.

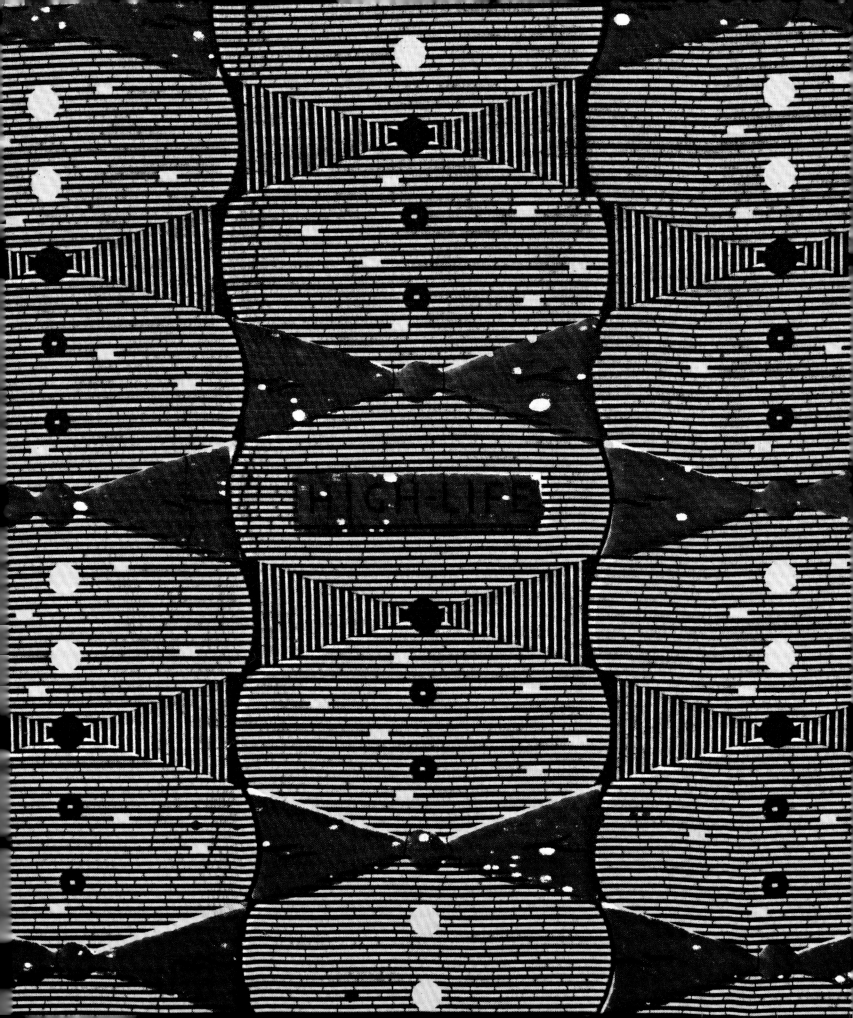

Fancy-printed cloth

Cotton

Chad/Central African Republic, 1996

113 x 137 cm

British Museum, 2011,2002.1

Printed by the *Compagnie Tchadienne de Textile*, this cloth was also made for sale in the Central African Republic. Although exhorting society at large to save and thus acquire credit, the cloth is in effect a walking advertisement for a particular company.

What's Our Story by Gloria Ojulari Sule
Mixed fabrics and other materials
London, UK, 2010
90 x 80 cm

Textile artwork commissioned by Brent
Museum and Archive, London in response
to the British Museum's touring exhibition
Fabric of a Nation. The artist describes her
work thus:

*The interactive costume designed for
two children to wear at the same time
is inspired by the bold and elaborate
Egungun Oyo masquerade costumes,
which are worn at festivals held by
Yoruba-speaking people in Nigeria to
remember and pay respect to ancestors.
The costume was also inspired by
Ghanaian* kente *and* adinkra *cloths,
traditional West African textiles and
contemporary African artwork. As with
traditional Egungun masquerade costumes,
the handmade piece has been made out of
a wide range of materials, from Dutch wax
prints to bottle tops, and from batik
fabrics to shells. The colourful strips of
cloth are made to move easily as wearers
dance and perform, and contain both
traditional and contemporary stories
which viewers or wearers are invited to
read and make up their own narratives
using the messages and images contained
within the costume.*[68]

KANGA, CAPULANA AND SHWESHWE: THE PRINTED CLOTH OF EASTERN AND SOUTHERN AFRICA

Keeper of the Rod by Karel Nel
Pastel and sprayed pigment on
bonded fibre fabric
South Africa, 1988
234 x 184 cm
Collection of Ms L. Goodman,
Johannesburg

At the centre of Nel's complex image are
the red, white and black printed textiles,
cheramine, worn by women of the
Comoros Islands at all the vital rites of
passage in their lives. They seem to infuse
all the other objects in the room with a
powerful spiritual charge.

Kanga, *capulana* and *shweshwe*: printed cloth of eastern and southern Africa

I am Kanga a gentle one that's me
I'm great and full of grace;
I'm the first when one is born
And definitely the last when death one faces.

A wedding cannot be without my presence –
Women wearing me are full of elegance.
At funerals the widow uses one,
Covering herself in the days she mourns
Girl in Qur'an classes must have me to adorn.[69]

FROM 'KANGA' BY MAHFOUDA ALLEY HAMID

These verses evoke the very special role played by the *kanga* in Swahili society, from birth to puberty, through courtship and marriage, to old age and death. *Kangas* are rectangular printed cloths, each with their own 'name' or inscription written in the same place in every design; they are sold and worn in matching pairs and are principally a woman's garment in Tanzania, Kenya and other countries of eastern Africa, though often worn singly by Maasai men at home and in public. They are also worn across the Arabian sea in Oman which has long-established connections with eastern Africa. *Kanga* is the Kiswahili word for the guinea-fowl and presumably the textiles were so named because the spotted patterns on the early cloths were reminiscent of the markings on the plumage of this bird. The term *leso* (which derives from the Portuguese *lenço*, meaning 'handkerchief' or 'scarf') is, however, still used in preference to *kanga* on the coast of Kenya.

In Somalia women wear black and white or red and white printed cloth known as *guntino*, without inscriptions or images, and in the Comoros Islands

Still **from** *The Nightingale*
by Grace Ndiritu, 2003

Using a single piece of printed cloth, the
artist wraps her face and head in many
different ways that suggest, among other
things, the infinite variety of messages –
from the personal to the universal – which
can be conveyed by the *kanga*.

women wear cloth, *cheramine*, with a similar pattern, which completely covers
their bodies and faces. In Mozambique the principal wrap-around garment is
the *capulana*, often worn with a headscarf, *lenço*, and tailored blouse, *quimau*,
while on Madagascar a cloth called *lamba hoany* has a very similar appearance
to *kanga*, including an inscription in Malagasy, yet is worn by men as well as
women outside the home. In Angola, men and women of the Herero people
wear the *samakaka*, a printed cloth a little like *kanga* but without an
inscription. In southern Africa, a complex history lies behind the discharge-
printed indigo cloth, commonly known as *shweshwe* (among Sotho and Zulu
speakers), *amajaman/ujamani* or more recently *idark* (among Xhosa-speakers)
or *amotoishi* (in Pedi) and sometimes 'German print'.[70] Most of these cloths
from eastern and southern Africa are now printed locally as well as overseas,
and there are interesting differences and similarities in the stories which have
surrounded their production.

Indigo cloth, particularly printed textiles from India known as *salempore*,
was traded along the southern African coast from at least the thirteenth

century, and there is some evidence that indigo dyeing of cloth was taking place in Botswana at this time.[71] Although worn by European settlers (particularly German and Swiss) from the fifteenth century onwards, *shweshwe* did not become widely worn by indigenous peoples in South Africa until the nineteenth century, partly as a result of increased missionary activity throughout the region at this time, and partly because it appears to have been adopted by King Moshoeshoe I (*c*.1786–1870) of the South Sotho people as a mark of pride and independence. The South African scholar Juliette Lieb du Toit[72] recounts an unconfirmed (but very plausible) legend that Moshoeshoe was given a substantial quantity of blue-print cloth and blankets by members of the Paris Evangelical Missionary society whom he had invited to stay in 1833 at his mountain stronghold of Thaba Bosiu. The subsequent popularity and assimilation of *shweshwe* and other imported textiles into black South African clothing was partly as a result of its association with charismatic figures such as Moshoeshoe, and partly because of its connotations of prestige and education, but also because of practical considerations such as the increasing costs of hide clothing following the rinderpest epidemics among cattle in eastern and southern Africa in the late nineteenth century.

The history of *kanga* and other types of dress worn further to the north on the Indian Ocean coast of Africa shows some similarities to that of *shweshwe* in South Africa, particularly as both textiles represented a means of asserting an independent, collective identity. The draped garments, *winda*, worn by both men and women in mid nineteenth-century eastern Africa were made of imported American cloth, *merikani* and later from British India after the American Civil War (1861–5) disrupted this trade.[73] In the 1870s women began dyeing this cloth in indigo to create a cloth known as *kaniki*, a name which is still used to describe cloth worn principally by women, though also by the *mganga* and their assistants, spirit healers and diviners who wear a combination of black, red and white *kaniki* as the distinctive uniform of their profession. During the 1860s it also became fashionable for ladies of high social status from Zanzibar and Mombasa to wear garments created by sewing together the printed *lenço* of a type which the Portuguese had first traded to eastern Africa in the sixteenth century but which, by the late nineteenth

Textile stamp
Wood
Lamu Island, Kenya, 1940s
13 x 16 x 5 cm
British Museum, Af2003,21.8

Early textiles, *kanga za mera*, were hand-stamped onto cloth using wooden blocks such as this one from Lamu Island, Kenya. The 'crosses and tangerines' design was particularly used on *kisutu*, the wedding *kanga*.

Women wearing the latest *kanga* fashions collect water at a well in late nineteenth century Zanzibar.

century, were being printed in Manchester, the Netherlands and Switzerland.

Nasra Mohammed Hilal of Malindi, Zanzibar, a journalist and radio broadcaster, told me that the sewing together of *lenço* to create a garment known as *leso ya kushona* was instigated by an Arab merchant of Zanzibar so that his wife could be completely covered when in public. However, Farouque Abdela, also of Zanzibar, suggests that this fashion began in Mombasa. Whether the fashion began in Zanzibar and spread to Mombasa or vice versa, during the late nineteenth century it encouraged local cloth traders to begin the practice of hand-stamping *merikani* cloths cut to the rectangular size of the sewn *lenço* strips; these hand-stamped textiles became known as *kanga za mera* and are recorded in several photos from the Zanzibar Archive[74] (see below).

By 1897, when slavery was officially abolished in eastern Africa, it is recorded that printed versions of the *kanga za mera* were being imported to Zanzibar from several printworks, including the former Newton Bank Printworks in Hyde, Manchester, UK, later to become ABC Printers, or A. Brunnschweiler & Co., which also began to export *shweshwe* to South Africa at this time.[75] This was a period of rapid and fundamental socio-political change for many communities in eastern and southern Africa – *kanga*, *shweshwe* and other printed cloths became one of the means through which

increased wealth and social status could be reflected.

Today the conventional form of the *kanga* is found mainly in Tanzania and Kenya, where those which are not imported from India or China are designed and printed in textile mills such as Rivatex at Eldoret in Kenya, and the Urafiki and Karibu textile companies in Dar Es Salaam, Urafiki being the first integrated mill in eastern Africa. There are also large textile factories at Kigali and Kisangani in neighbouring Rwanda and the Democratic Republic of Congo from where many printed textiles, particularly *kitenge* cloth, are imported into Uganda.[76]

Most *kanga* designs are initially hand-painted, the artist producing a single section, usually a quarter, which is then adjusted or embellished on a computer before being transferred onto a nickel plate prior to roller printing. They are then sold in pairs to Swahili women who will cut, hem and sometimes tailor them into dresses and other clothes. Although in a sense *kangas* have, therefore, gone from being an indication of high social status to a commodity

Kangas are worn in different styles to suit particular occasions or moods. One style, known as *ushungi*, is used when walking along the beach, as here at Bagamoyo in Tanzania, with one *kanga* wrapped tightly around the head; at home this headdress is removed and is draped loosely around the shoulders.

which is much more widely available, the number, price and quality of *kangas* owned by a woman is still very much an indication of her status in society. Those printed in the mills of Urafiki and Karibu in Tanzania are generally of better quality – and correspondingly more expensive – than those imported from India.

A new-born baby may be wrapped in an uncut and unstitched pair of *kangas* to confer prosperity, strength and beauty on the child and as a symbol of the parents' love for their offspring. In this case the *mji* or 'town', the central space and design of the *kanga*, may take on an element of the second meaning of *mji* in Kiswahili – 'the womb'. Young girls who have begun to menstruate will be given a *kanga* of red and black to wear; at their puberty ceremonies they will also give a *kanga* to their *somo*, a 'ritual mother' who has trained them in the requirements of adult womanhood. Certain *kangas*, usually of the *kisutu* 'crosses and tangerines' pattern (see p. 107) first worn at marriage, are used specifically for praying in the mosque. These *kangas* are often those which have previously been used at the funerals of women to cover the corpse while it is washed, after which the *kangas* are sent to the mosque where their use by female worshippers continues to bless and honour the deceased.

Kangas very much reflect changing times, fashions and tastes, providing a detailed chronology of the social, political, religious, emotional and sexual concerns of those who wear them. Their patterns and inscriptions also vary according to the age of the wearer and the context in which the cloth is worn. The unspoken language of the *kanga* provides a way of suggesting thoughts and feelings which cannot be said out loud, and of relieving suspicions and anxieties which inevitably arise. *Kangas* regularly move between the realms of the secular and the sacred. They play a central role in all the major rite-of-passage ceremonies in a Swahili woman's life, and yet may be used for the most mundane of functions. It is this ambivalence which makes *kanga* cloth almost emblematic of multi-faceted Swahili society.

Mimi kama kanga: nafa na uzuri wangui
'I am like a *kanga*: I die in all my beauty'
SWAHILI SONG[77]

Printed cloth (*kanga*)
Cotton
Tanzania, 2002
117 x 166 cm
British Museum, Af2002,09.17

The inscription on this *kanga* from
Tanzania reads, 'The new millennium
belongs to us'. The central space, known
as *mji*, meaning 'town' or 'womb', is left
deliberately empty except for the deep
blue of the unknown future.

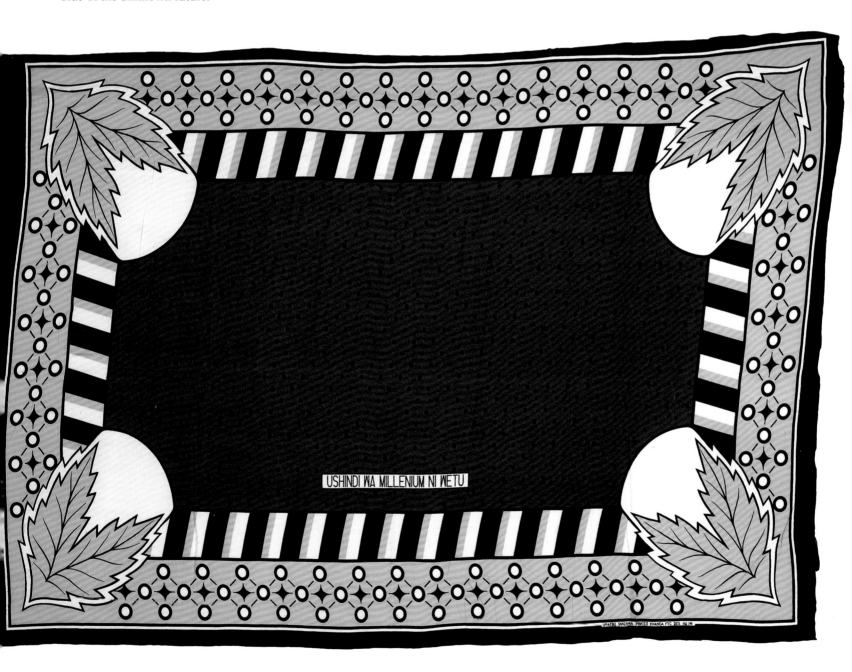

USHINDI WA MILLENIUM NI WETU

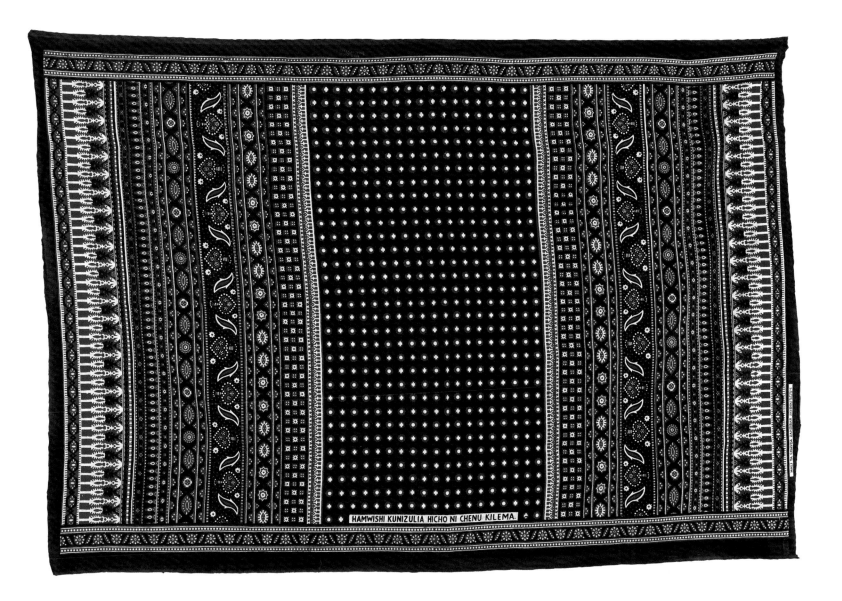

Printed cloth (*kanga*)
Cotton
Tanzania, 2002
110 x 160 cm
British Museum, Af2002,09.6

Kangas of this design and colour have been worn at weddings for generations and are known as *kisutu*. Originally these *kangas* had no inscription, but today they often carry one and are printed in a variety of colours. This one reads: HAMWISHI KUNIZULIA HICHO NI CHENU KILEMA, 'Your problem is that you can't stop backbiting'. Worn by the bride and her friends and family, the inscription serves as a warning to anyone who might have a problem with any aspect of the marriage. The central panel displays the 'crosses and tangerines' pattern characteristic of wedding *kangas*.

Printed handkerchief (*lenço*)

Cotton

Comoros Islands, mid 20th century

74 x 76 cm

British Museum, Af2002,09.10

Printed handkerchief, *lenço*, from the
Comoros Islands and of a type traded by
the Portuguese along the eastern African
coast since the sixteenth century.

**Somali woman wearing a printed cloth,
late 19th century**

This photograph taken in the 1880s shows
a Somali woman wearing a printed cloth,
the design of which derives from the
practice of sewing together six *lenço*. This
early form of patterning (with six square
design elements on a single cloth) is still
used on cloth worn in southern Somalia,
where it is known as *guntino*, and in the
Comoros Islands, where it is known as
cheramine. In the Comoros Islands the
practice of sewing together individual
lenço has only disappeared within the last
few decades. It appears that this type of
patterning remained popular in these more
conservative societies at the northern and
southern extremities of the Indian Ocean
coast of Africa, while *kanga* underwent a
number of metamorphoses in the central
region, particularly around cosmopolitan
centres of commerce such as Mombasa
and Zanzibar.

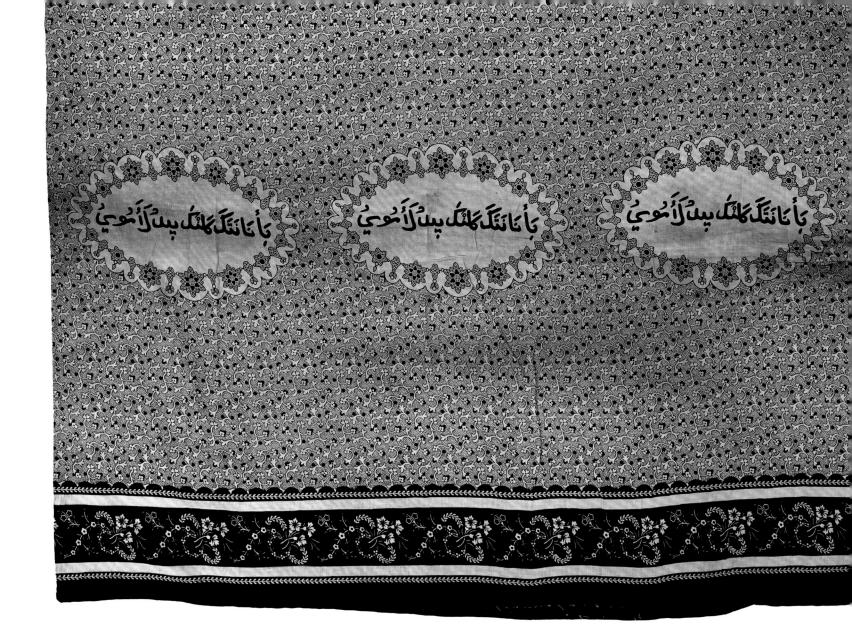

Printed cloth (*kanga*) (detail)
Cotton
Lamu Island, Kenya, early 20th century
111 x 162 cm
British Museum, Af1914,0417.1

Although varieties of *kanga* began to be worn from the 1870s, in the early 1900s the familiar size, shape and pattern of today's *kanga* began to develop. Nasra Hilal explained to me that the first 'complete' *kanga* had no borders in its design. A later development included borders, *pindo*, along the top and bottom of the rectangle, and finally on all four sides enclosing a space known as *mji*, 'the town'.[78] These early *kangas* were printed solely in red and/or black on a white ground; the inclusion of a Kiswahili proverb or saying written in the Arabic script, as in this example acquired in 1914, was a slightly later addition. The inscription reads BWANA, NATAKA KANGA, PONDA LA MOYO, which roughly translates as 'My husband, I want a *kanga* which is my heart's desire'.

Printed cloth (*kanga*)
Cotton
Kenya, early 20th century
108 x 332 cm
British Museum, Af2003,21.19

There is often a subtle link between the pattern and motifs employed on the *kanga* and its inscription. For example, this *kanga* has a design of *zingifuri* fruit running around its border and an inscription which reads: USIONE NI KIMYA NINA MENGI, 'I may be quiet but there's a lot in my heart'. The *zingifuri* fruit has a prickly exterior, but its flesh is used for a variety of social and cultural activities including the colouring of food, dyeing of grasses used in matting, colouring the hair and even for the Hindu caste mark.

Fine Art students taught by B. M. Maganga at the Bagamoyo College of Arts in Tanzania must learn various methods of designing *kangas* throughout their course, graduating from geometrical designs in years one and two to more complex floral and 'cultural' motifs in their final year.

Right **Printed cloth (*kanga*)**
Cotton
Tanzania, early 21st century
110 x 163 cm
British Museum, Af2002,09.13

Kangas may carry political or educational messages, though the HIV epidemic seems to have driven away some of these didactic texts, replacing them with exhortations to fight the disease or to put trust in God and not set too much store by worldly goods. This *kanga* from Tanzania has an inscription which reads, 'We young people declare war against HIV and AIDS because we have the capacity and the will to do it'.

Printed cloth (*kanga*)
Cotton
Tanzania, 2003
106 x 166 cm
British Museum, Af2003,21.4

The inscription on this *kanga* from Tanzania reads, 'The mangos are ready', an invitation from wife to husband to help himself. For almost a century the proverbs and sayings (*methali*) which appear on *kangas* have been an essential part of their design and appeal. Manufacturers and traders, whether in Africa, India, China or in Europe, have learned that they must consult and sometimes pay their customers to suggest the most appropriate inscriptions and topical designs for the *kangas* they produce, knowing that if they do not, or if they try to exploit their customers in any other way, eastern African women will quickly advise them of their mistake, or simply refuse to buy or wear their product.

Tailored blouse (*quimau*)
Cotton
Isla de Mozambique, Mozambique, mid 20th century
31 x 117 cm
British Museum, Af2008,2012.2

A tailored blouse (*quimau*) with embroidered collar trimmed with lace and small patch pockets, from the Isla de Mozambique.

Below right Early 20th century photograph of Makua women from Angoche, Mozambique, wearing *capulana*s, *lenço* and *quimau*. Those with white faces are wearing the medicinal mask, *musiro*.

MWEMBE TAYARI

Printed cloth (*samakaka*)
Cotton
Herero people, Angola, 2012
Private collection

Herero men and women of Angola wear a printed cloth
(*samakaka*) on special occasions including initiation,
marriage and at funerals. The Herero of Angola dress in a
different way to Herero living in Namibia and Botswana.
The colours red, black and gold reflect those of the
Angolan national flag.

Herero woman of Mahalapye, Botswana in 1959. She is wearing an early nineteenth century European style dress made of *shweshwe*. The various designs on imported cloth rapidly acquired local names in southern Africa: the circular motif with floral insert, such as that on this dress, became known as *lehlolakgomo*, 'the eye of the cow'.[79]

Printed cloth (*shweshwe*) (detail)
Cotton
King William's Town, South Africa, 2008
92 x 101 cm
British Museum, 2008,2012.8

The production of *shweshwe* moved to South Africa in the late 1980s when the firm Da Gama bought rollers from ABC in Manchester, UK, and set up a printworks situated at Zwelitsha in the Eastern Cape (near King William's Town). The 'three cats' trademark label (shown here) distinguishes it from the many imitations of authentic discharge-printed *shweshwe* on the market.

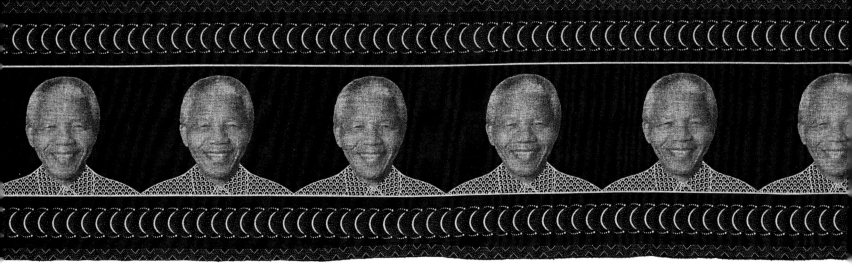

Printed cloth (*shweshwe*) (detail)
Cotton
King William's Town, South Africa, 2008
89 x 193 cm
British Museum, 2008,2012.12

Although a standard range of patterns
has remained popular in southern Africa,
innovations are regularly introduced,
some inspired by traditional mural motifs,
others featuring images, such as this one
of former president Nelson Mandela.

Herero woman of Botswana ironing a
dress of *shweshwe*.

Process working drawing for
Africa Rifting Bloodlines
by Georgia Papageorge
Mixed media on canvas
South Africa, 2008
230 x 140 cm

The South African artist Georgia
Papageorge uses cloth in a variety of
innovative ways in her films, paintings and
three-dimensional installations. In this
sketch she uses three types of cloth –
Scottish tartan, 'German print' (*shweshwe*)
and American red cotton sheeting
(*merikani*) – all of which have been
assimilated by African peoples into their
own systems of thought and culture. In so
doing she suggests a meeting of minds and
hearts after the divisions of the recent past.
This is a process working drawing for the
'Washing line' event at the village of Enon,
Eastern Cape in July 2007, part of the
Africa Rifting Bloodlines series by
Papageorge. Students from different parts
of South Africa were invited to attach cloth
to the lines as a symbol of interaction
between different peoples and the
destruction of barriers. Attached are pieces
of *shweshwe* indigo cloth, Scottish tartan,
which has been widely adopted by peoples
in eastern and southern Africa (see p. 240),
red 'Maasai' blanket and the red and white
chevron cloth which the artist uses to
suggest division or prohibition elsewhere
in her work, but in this context suggesting
the removal of barriers.[80]

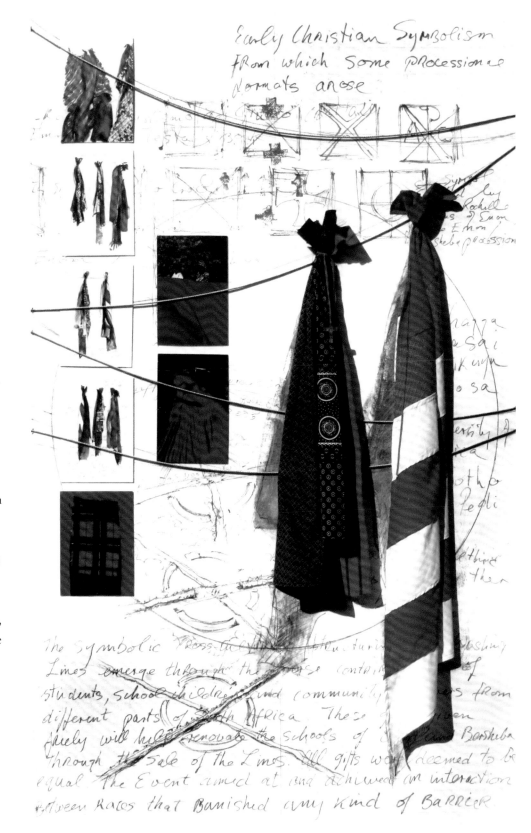

Printed cloth (*lamba hoany*)
Cotton
Madagascar, early 21st century
160 x 105 cm
British Museum, Af2006,05.1,
donated by Polly Savage

The inscription reads, 'There is an end to everything'. Human beings, like prawns in the sea, live a brief and transitory existence which could be ended at any moment.

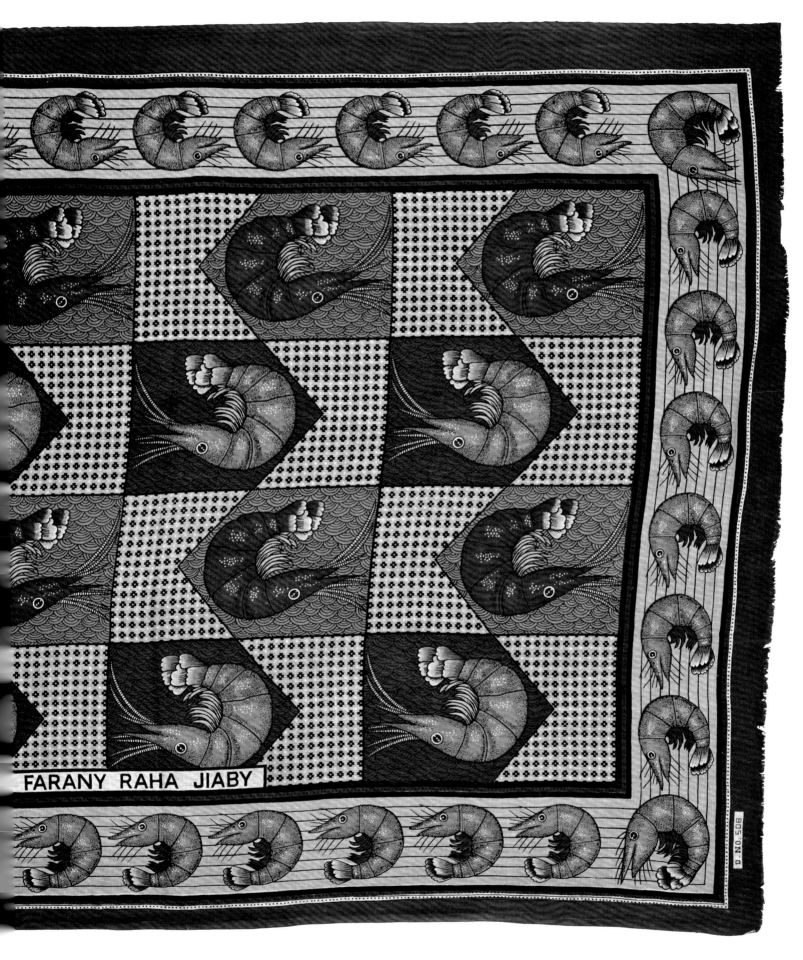

FARANY RAHA JIABY

D. NO. 805.

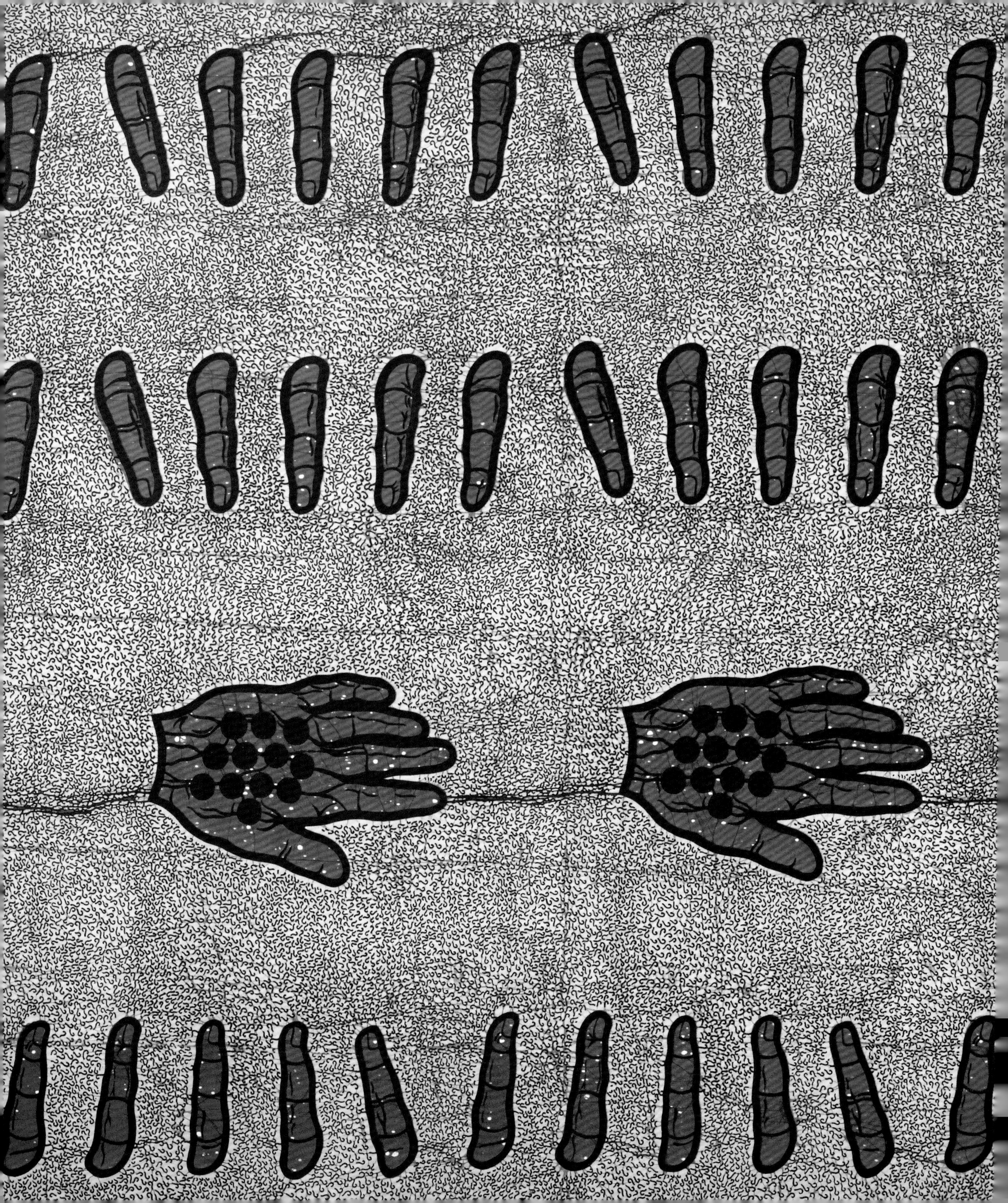

TEXTILES AND TRADE

Wax-printed cloth (detail)
Cotton
Netherlands/West Africa, 1980s
118 x 183 cm
British Museum, 2011,2002.84

One of the earliest designs of 'wax' print cloth created in Europe for trade to West Africa was the 'fingers and hand'. The cloth is a visual reminder of a popular proverb, which roughly translates as, 'Fingers on their own are not much use, but together they make a hand – and money'. In other words, 'Work together and you will be successful'. In this case the money is represented by the twelve pennies that made one shilling in the old pre-decimal British coinage. There may also be a religious perspective in this image, suggested by Jesus holding his twelve disciples in his hand.

Textiles and trade

Then we travelled thence by sea for fifteen nights and arrived at Maqdashaw [Mogadishu] *... Its people are powerful merchants. In it are manufactured the cloths named after it which have no rival, and are transported as far as Egypt and elsewhere.*[81]
IBN BATTUTA, AD 1331 (AH 731)

It appears Nigeria, and many parts of fashion-savvy Africa, have taken over other people's inventions [fabrics], *improved on them and re-presented them to the world.*[82]
TOYIN ODULATE

In early 2011 I was working in the National Museum of Art in Maputo, Mozambique. Across the road from the Museum was a small shop selling textiles. 'Hausa,' said my friend Ademola Oshin from Nigeria, who was working with me. 'Hausa?' I queried, thinking it was a long way to come to run a small shop in Maputo. 'Yes, I bet you that shop is run by a Hausa guy from Nigeria'. A couple of days later we visited the shop – Ade was right.

From the earliest time at which cloth became a suitable commodity to trade, certain peoples in different parts of Africa made this activity their profession, gradually building up trading networks, which each generation would build upon and expand. In West Africa the Hausa and Dyula (referred to as 'Mandinga' in early accounts) are renowned traders in cloth and other commodities, crossing national and even international boundaries to seek new markets for their goods. In fact, the Hausa cloth trader in Maputo had travelled a relatively small distance compared to another Hausa trader, Issifi Mayaki, who travelled to New York City in 1992 with his goods and set up a table in the West 125th street market near the Apollo Theatre. When that market was closed by the authorities, he relocated to the Malcolm Shabazz Harlem Market on West 116th Street. In his book *Money Has No Smell:*

The Africanization of New York City, Paul Stoller[83] recounts Mayaki's story and those of numerous other African traders who have built up international networks over the years in New York, though it is a story which is also played out in London, Paris and many other cities of the world. By the same token, successful cloth traders in India and China have set up businesses in Africa, first in the great towns of eastern Africa such as Mombasa and Dar Es Salaam, but more recently in West Africa. One of the foremost cloth trading families in Mombasa are the Kaderdinas, whose ancestor, Kaderdina Haji Essak, came from Kutch in northern India and set up his business, Mali Ya Abdulla, which today thrives in Biashara Street, Mombasa (see p. 129). Kaderdina's great-great-grandson still designs the textiles in Mombasa before sending them to India for printing, though – as we have seen throughout this book, particularly in Chapters Three and Four – it is a trade driven entirely by African taste and patronage.

Girl selling Senegalese mats in a Paris market in 2010 (AH 1431). She is wearing a T-shirt designed by the artist Hassan Hajjaj, who also took the photograph.

From an early date cloth, together with shells such as cowries and metal manillas and ingots of various forms, had been the main currency of trade. Even after the widespread introduction of minted coinage, these former 'currencies' continue to hold a particular significance in African societies. Cloth is relatively light and durable, and could be rolled or wound into easily transportable forms. It is likely that the characteristic narrow-strip weaving of West Africa developed partly because of the ease with which its product could be traded. A large wheel of cloth could easily be cut into strips and sewn together into a number of individual textiles, thus precluding the need to trade entire cloths, which would have to be folded or stored in ways that would make them more susceptible to damage. Likewise the raffia palm leaf, which provides the raw material for many of the textiles of central Africa, was woven into relatively small sections dictated by the length of the palm mid-rib from which fibres were stripped. All the larger cloths of this region are made from smaller sections sewn together, sections which could be traded easily in tightly wound bundles or 'books' of a given number of square raffia cloths.[84]

In the early sixteenth century, Portuguese merchants described the vigorous trade in raffia cloth taking place in the ancient Kingdom of Kongo at the mouth of the great Congo River system, the waterway which helped to make this trade possible.[85] The Portuguese were the first Europeans to navigate the coast of Africa, from the Mediterranean down the Atlantic coast to the Gulf of Guinea, then south around the Cape of Good Hope into the Indian Ocean and up the eastern African coast to Zanzibar, Mombasa and Lamu Island. Everywhere they went they found a thriving import and export trade in textiles, which in many cases had been established for centuries before their coming. This trade included locally made cloth, cloth imported from other parts of Africa and, in some cases, cloth imported from different parts of the world.

From at least the eighth century, regular trans-Saharan caravans brought textiles and other goods from North Africa, the Mediterranean and beyond to the upper reaches of the Niger and thence to the forest kingdoms of West Africa and the coast. When the Portuguese began to navigate the West African coast in the late fifteenth century, they quickly discovered that local people, despite their own sophisticated textile traditions, had a great liking for cloth of North African inspiration. This was a taste which the Portuguese rapidly set about exploiting, initially by setting up what amounted to textile 'factories' in Oran and elsewhere in Morocco to make cloth for the West African trade.[86] Today we may think that declining standards caused by mass production are a particularly modern malaise, but it is interesting to note that as early as 1510 there were complaints made by local people to the Portuguese trading post at El Mina (in modern day Ghana) that the quality of Oran cloth had declined for precisely that same reason.[87]

Some cloths of North African pattern and manufacture were even traded around the Cape to Sofala at the mouth of the Zambesi River, though long before the coming of the Portuguese on the Indian Ocean coast, Africa had looked to Arabia, India and China for its textile trade, both in complete cloths and raw materials for weaving (as it still does today in many respects). Throughout Africa, trade has been a primary factor in driving innovation in existing traditions and in initiating new ones, sometimes involving textiles from other parts of the world which have been transformed by African taste, imagination and invention. It is a process that shows no sign of slowing down, even in the face of world recession.

Adinkrahene Nana Kwaku Duah II's shop at Ntonso, Asante region, Ghana, 2010. The *adinkrahene* is the head of the guild of *adinkra* carvers and cloth makers.

Roll of cloth currency
Raffia
Mbuun people, Democratic Republic
of Congo, early 20th century
86 x 11 cm
British Museum, Af1910,0420.350

Cloth, whether locally produced or
imported from elsewhere in Africa or from
overseas, was an important currency in
Africa before minted coins came into
common use in the twentieth century. This
tightly rolled bale of raffia palm leaf cloth
was collected for the British Museum
among the Mbuun people of the southern
Congo Basin by Emil Torday in 1910.

Rolls of 'wax' and 'fancy' printed cloth for sale at Treichville market, Abidjan, Ivory Coast in 1963. The bowl filled with rolls of cloth (in the left foreground) would be carried on the head by women transporting cloth from one place to another in the market. Such bowls of cloth also became a symbol of chiefly power and prestige, particularly among the Akan-speaking peoples of West Africa, so that whenever a chief appears in public he is often preceded by a woman carrying cloth in this way, as well as by sword-bearers and other officials (see pp. 74–5).

Hand-painted *kanga* designs and instructions
Paper and cardboard
Dar Es Salaam, Tanzania, mid 20th century
British Museum, 2012,2026.1, donated by James and MacKenzie Ryan

One of the great *kanga* designers and traders of eastern Africa was Mr K. G. Peera who died in Dar Es Salaam in 2011, at the age of 99. Initially based in Zanzibar, he wrote his design instructions in his native Gujarati (see illustration) which his brother translated into English and sent to the firm C. ITOH in Japan for printing. In 1964 Peera fled the revolution on Zanzibar with nothing but his suitcase of *kanga* designs, settling in Dar Es Salaam for the rest of his life. His affectionate Kiswahili nickname was *Miwanimdogo*, 'Little Spectacles'. The illustration shows one of Peera's 1960s designs. The wording along the selvage in the bottom left corner reads:
REG, DESIGN FOR K. G. Peera (MIWANIMDOGO) C. ITOH KHANGA.

Printed cloth (*kanga*)
Cotton
Mombasa, Kenya, 2003
104 x 164 cm
British Museum, Af2003,21.5

The inscription on this *kanga* reads, 'The evening sun can't dry the rice', meaning that the wife is not very happy with her husband's performance in bed. Certain themes have probably changed very little over the years, especially those concerning the liaisons in which the *kanga* has always played a part, particularly in the context of intimate social and sexual relationships and marriage. In Mombasa the great-grandson of Kaderdina Haji Essak, the founder of the textile business in the nineteenth century, still creates designs such as this, which are sent to India for printing before being returned to Mombasa for sale.

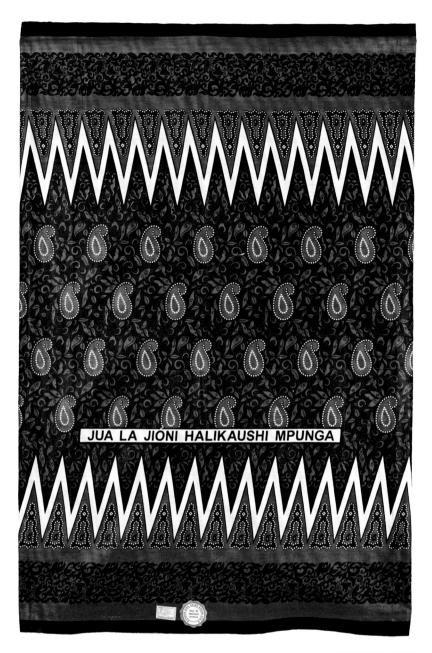

Unloading *kangas* at Mali Ya Abdulla, the shop of the Kaderdina family in Biashara Street, Mombasa.

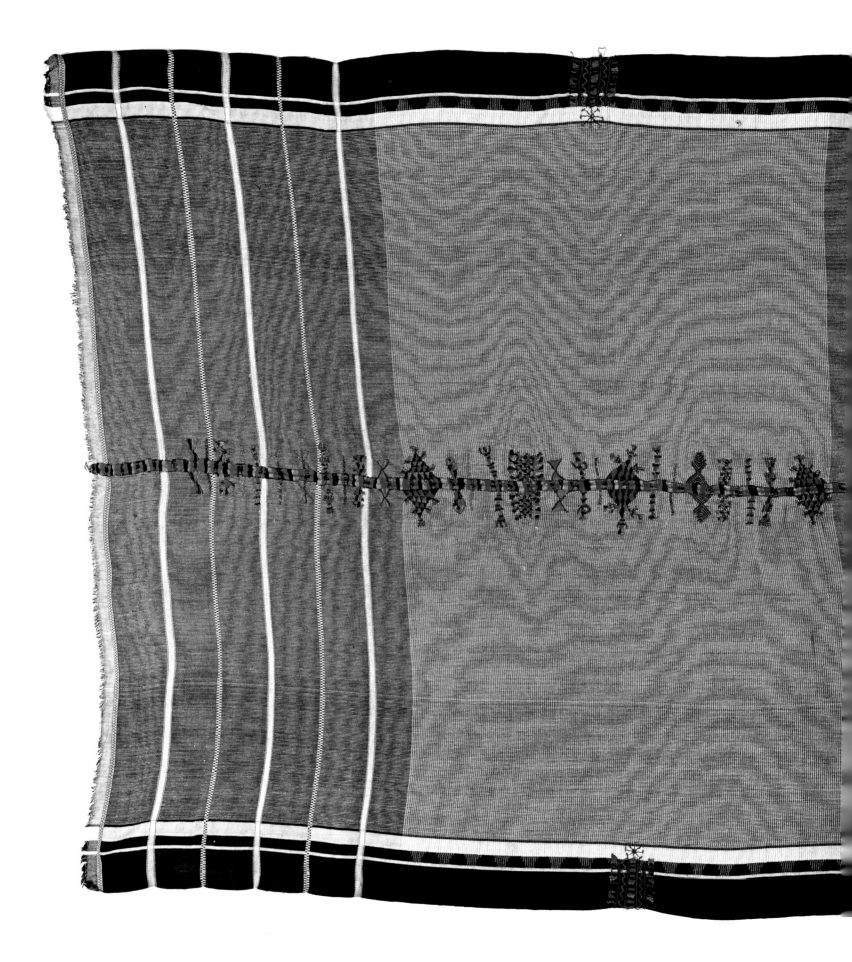

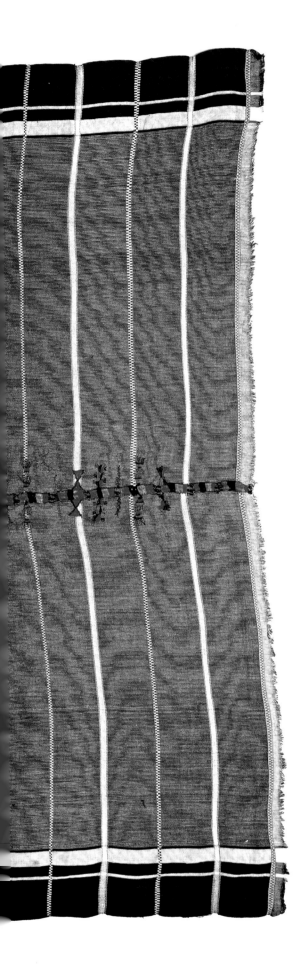

Woman's shawl (*derfudit*)
Cotton, silk
Kerdassa/Siwa Oasis, Egypt,
late 20th century
222 x 165 cm
British Museum, Af1988,07.2

For many centuries weavers in the village of Kerdassa, just outside Cairo in northern Egypt, would produce cloth such as this blue and white shawl (*derfudit*), for trade via desert caravan to the remote oasis of Siwa in Egypt's Western Desert. The shawls were subsequently embroidered by women in Siwa, using silk thread which would also have been traded from Cairo or from neighbouring Libya.[88] The red, yellow and orange silk represents the colour of ripening dates, Siwa's most important cash crop, but may also suggest the colours of the sun. Siwa has a connection with the ancient Egyptian sun god, Amun–Re.

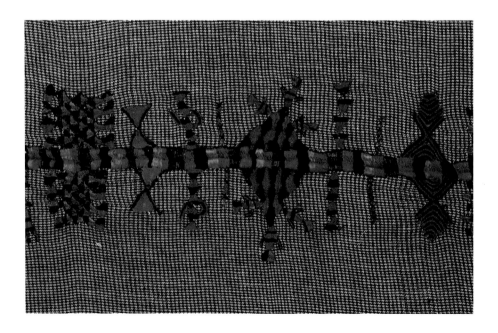

Narrow-strip cloth (*aso oke*)
Cotton, silk
Yoruba people, Nigeria, late 19th century
111 x 181 cm
British Museum, Af1900,–.36, donated by Dr Coker Adams

This late nineteenth-century cloth, woven by a Yoruba weaver in Nigeria, is composed of ten narrow strips of silk and cotton embellished with a Qur'an board motif. The European magenta silk waste used in this cloth is known as *alhaari* and was a regular item of trade from the oases of southern Tunisia and Libya. Many of the woven and embroidered textiles from this region show similarities to textiles of northern Nigeria, reflecting a long tradition of trans-Saharan trade. This cloth is an early example of *aso oke*, or 'high status cloth', woven and worn by the Yoruba in ever-changing varieties of pattern, colour and material.

Lace *aso ebi*

Women at a wedding in Benin City, Nigeria, dressed in *aso ebi* uniform ensembles of imported lace fabric. *Aso ebi* is the Yoruba name for matching outfits worn by groups of friends or relations at important events such as weddings or funerals – or even at parties. Industrially produced 'lace' embroideries, initially from the Austrian province of Vorarlberg and from Switzerland, became extremely popular in post-independence southern Nigeria and remain so today. In common with imitation Javanese batik 'wax' prints in West Africa, 'German print' or *shweshwe* in southern Africa, and Scottish tartan in eastern Africa, lace has become a very Nigerian expression of a tradition from another part of the world.[89]

Patterned cloth
Cotton
Igbo people, Akwete Village, Nigeria,
early 20th century
192 x 110 cm
British Museum, Af1934,0307.119,
donated by Charles A. Beving

Woven by a female weaver in the Igbo
village of Akwete in south-eastern Nigeria,
this type of cloth was originally modelled
on certain high-status cloths of the Yoruba
of Ijebu-Ode (see p. 197), but made for
sale to wealthy Ijo clients, principally in
the trading ports of New Calabar, Brass,
Bonny and Okrika. A legendary weaver
known as Dada Nwakata is believed to
have started the Akwete weaving tradition
in the late nineteenth century, many of the
designs (which she jealously guarded)
coming to her in visions or through
dreams. Other weavers did not take up
the tradition until after her death.[90] The
patterns and colours of Akwete cloth are
extremely diverse, so much so that it is
rare to find two with even approximately
similar designs. The design of this
particular cloth is said to have been
inspired by the pattern of falling leaves.

'Cut-thread cloth' (*pelete bite*)
Cotton
Kalabari people, Nigeria, late 20th century
89 x 171 cm
British Museum, Af1981,11.8

This type of cloth is known as *pelete bite*, literally 'cut-thread cloth', and was created by a Kalabari woman of southern Nigeria. Using imported Indian cotton cloth, known variously among the Kalabari as Madras, *injiri* or George, the makers cut and remove threads from the original structure of the cloth to create the design. The imported cloth has a weave structure of sufficient density to support this technique without unravelling. The principal motif on this cloth is *etemi*, 'the wineglass stem', though the Kalabari have a wide range of motifs. *Pelete bite* cloths are worn at important events, including ceremonies marking birth, marriage and death.[91]

A stall selling rolls of Manjak cloth at HLM market, Dakar, Senegal, 2006. HLM stands for *Habitations á loyer modéré*, 'Affordable rent housing', an arrondissement or division of the city of Dakar in which public housing was available and where the textile market has expanded steadily since it was opened in 1976.

Narrow-strip cloth (*pano d'obra*) (detail)
Cotton
Manjak people, Guinea-Bissau, early 20th century
115 x 206 cm
British Museum, Af1934,0307.195, donated by Charles A. Beving

When the Portuguese first navigated the Guinea Coast of West Africa they found that local people had a great taste for textiles of North African Amazigh (Berber) manufacture or inspiration, a taste which had been fed by access to textiles traded across the Sahara, or woven on the southern fringes of the desert by weavers familiar with the patterning of trade cloths from the north. The Portuguese initially set up workshops in Morocco to cater for this trade, though that of course meant shipping the finished products many hundreds of miles from the Mediterranean to the Gulf of Guinea. The Portuguese therefore enslaved Wolof and Manding weavers, from the regions which are now Senegal and Guinea Bissau, and took them to the Cape Verde islands. There they were taught to weave the intricately patterned cloths which were popular in the Hispano-Mauresque civilization (tenth to fifteenth centuries AD) in southern Spain and North Africa. These textiles assimilated the patterning of Amazigh (Berber) cloths (woven by women on upright, single-heddle looms) but were woven by men on complex, multi-heddle 'draw looms' which required additional sets of pulleys to be operated by 'draw boys' positioned on either side of the weaver. Later this style of weaving, though adapted to the West African narrow-strip loom, transferred to the mainland and can still be found today among Manjak and Papel weavers of Senegambia, who use a small draw loom with just one 'draw boy' working with the weaver. Similar looms are also still used in the town of Mahdia in Tunisia and share a common ancestor in the great draw looms of the past.[92]

Blanket (*kaasa landaka*) (detail)
Wool, goat hair
Fulbe people, Mali, late 20th century
255 x 141 cm
British Museum, Af2006,23.12

Wool and goat hair blankets such as this are known as *kaasa landaka* and are woven by male Fulbe weavers in the region of the central Niger Delta. This is where, historically, the great trans-Saharan caravans would transfer their goods to the trading networks of the river. The cloths are woven in a characteristically West African technique of six strips, which are sewn together to make the completed cloth. The designs and patterning, however, are of North African inspiration, though the Amazigh (Berber) cloths which display similar patterns would have been woven by women on upright, single-heddle looms that produce one continuous piece of cloth. These cloths are still highly prized by peoples of the forest regions to the south, such as the Asante of Ghana, who themselves weave the most sumptuous textiles. In Asante the proverb *woda kaasa so?*, 'Do you sleep on *kaasa*?', asks whether you really are a man of the highest standing – or just boasting.[93]

The main motif is called *landal* – hence the name *landaka*. The textile is composed of six strips, and the two *landal* motifs on the two central strips are arranged back to back to create a design called *sudu misiide*, 'the mosque'.

Asafo banner
Cotton, silk
Fante people, Ghana, 19th century
123 x 180 cm
British Museum, Af1978,22.715

The Fante *asafo* companies or 'war people'
of coastal Ghana were initially formed as
competitive military organizations
controlling the vital ports and landing
places used by Europeans trading along the
coast. They often acted as middlemen
between the Europeans and powerful
African kingdoms inland such as Asante.
Today the *asafo* companies are still highly
competitive, but have taken on the role of
socio-political organizations representing

particular interests and communities.

Throughout their history the Fante
asafo adopted some of the military
organization and regalia of the Europeans,
including the pivotal importance of the flag
or banner as an identifying symbol, a
rallying point and an object of pride and
high esteem within a particular military
division or unit. The imagery of the *asafo*
banners, while maintaining some elements
of their European models (such as the
Union flag), were adapted to reflect local
wisdom and proverbial language which
could be understood by the Fante but not
by the Europeans. Most banners proclaim
the strength of the particular *asafo* they
represent – and the weaknesses of an

opposing company. In this nineteenth-
century banner, the left-hand side
summarizes the strengths of the company
it represents. The figure on the left, holding
a sword in one hand and scales in the
other, signifies control of the gold trade.
The elephant with its trunk around a palm
tree signifies either the strength of the
elephant, or possibly the strength of the
palm tree which the elephant cannot pull
down, though both the elephant and the
palm tree represent trade goods: ivory and
palm oil. To the right of the tree the crow
in the top right corner is a standard symbol
of revulsion in *asafo* banners, and the big
cat immediately beneath it must represent
an opposing company.[94]

TEXTILES, STATUS AND LEADERSHIP

Woman's waist cloth (detail)
Raffia
Dida people, Ivory Coast,
mid 20th century
40 x 99 cm
British Museum, Af1963,13.37

Such cloths are worn by women to signal
their descent from a long line of nobility.
(See pp. 150–51 for full caption.)

Textiles, status and leadership

Orí adétù ńpète àrán, orí adáranan ńpète àtijọba

The head that wears a cloth cap, ẹtù, strives to wear a velvet cap; the one that wears a velvet cap strives to wear the crown of a king.[95]

YORUBA PROVERB

Textiles, more than any other art form in Africa, represent a means of declaring status and of exercising leadership. There are, of course, innumerable fields in which status can be inherited or achieved in society – through royalty and nobility, politics, religion, the military, artistry and craftsmanship, to name but a few – and usually a degree of leadership is required by those who are in positions of authority in these walks of life. Textiles in their many forms – dress, regalia, wall and floor coverings, flags, banners, animal trappings, tents and even coffins – offer ways of defining, reinforcing and actively carrying out these roles in many of Africa's hugely diverse societies.

In pre-colonial Africa, centralized kingdoms and empires such as Asante in West Africa, Ethiopia in north-east Africa, Kuba in central Africa and Imerina in Madagascar developed a pyramid structure of officials and title-holders in political, religious and military roles, all of whom were ultimately answerable to the king or emperor. Dress and regalia were an outward and visible way of defining these roles – and to a considerable extent are still so today. Although military and political power may have been transferred to the governments of modern nation states, the spiritual, religious and social significance of pre-colonial kingdoms, chiefdoms, priesthoods and faiths remains as powerful as ever throughout Africa. The way in which individual or collective status and leadership is communicated within these different structures is often mediated by cloth.

The spiritual and secular elements of leadership are often combined in one person and reflected in the finery of the ruler's dress; although sometimes, as in the case of Muhammad Ahmad, the Sufi religious leader or Mahdi ('rightly guided one') in late nineteenth-century Sudan, dress may be deliberately austere to reflect a disdain for worldly goods. Often colour plays a particularly important role in distinguishing certain kinds of spiritual and religious leadership, such as the red cloth worn by the *mganga* or spirit healer of eastern Africa, or the predominantly blue clothing of certain Zionist preachers of southern Africa. In both cases – though this is admittedly a generalized assessment of a highly complex area of research – such colours represent the particular abilities of these spiritual leaders to occupy a mediating role between conflicting supernatural forces.

Cloth is not only worn or displayed as a symbol of power by African leaders, but also accumulated and given as a reward to those who have performed particular services. In the Ethiopian Empire of the eighteenth and nineteenth centuries, the Keeper of the Silk Caves was one of the highest officials in the land and was responsible for the emperor's vast supplies of raw and woven silk, imported mainly from China. Sometimes the only true measure of a man's status in life is revealed after his death, as is still the case among the Kuba people of the Kasai region of the southern Congo Basin, when fine cloth which a chief or high-ranking official has accumulated throughout his life is shown to a wider public for the first time at his funeral.[96] Similarly, among the Merina nobility of Madagascar, the finest silk cloth (*lamba mena*) was used as a shroud to wrap the body of the deceased, and an additional shroud of elaborately patterned silk (*lamba akotofahana*) would be used when the body was exhumed for the 'second-burial' rituals, *famadihana*.[97] Among the Bwende peoples of southern Democratic Republic of Congo, anthropomorphic fabric

coffins, *niombo*, are created for dead chiefs from imported red blankets associated with chieftaincy, leadership and power. A related tradition exists among the neighbouring Bembe people (see p. 38) who make ancestor figures covered with prestigious cloth which are kept in houses and given sustenance as if they are living members of the family.[98] The *koma* ancestor figures of the Giriama people of Kenya are fed and clothed in a similar way (see above).

Cloth has always been synonymous with wealth and power in Africa. In many regions the most important symbol of status for women is the dress worn at or associated with marriage, and subsequently worn at important events or ceremonies. The male equivalent is the voluminous gown or cape, often embroidered or embellished with luxury materials, patterns and attachments. These dresses and gowns, together with certain types of cloth, such as *kente* in West Africa and *kanga* in eastern Africa, which were once monopolized by ruling elites, have become much more widely worn and as such have become symbols of enfranchisement and freedom. However, it is by celebrating and

Left A Giriama man of coastal Kenya giving *pombe*, or millet beer, to figures which represent ancestors, *koma*, both male and female, who ensure the continuing good fortune of their living descendants. The ancestors not only insist that they are given food and drink at the same time as the rest of the family, but also that they are dressed correctly. Male figures wear scraps of cloth representing *bafta*, a white garment which covers the upper part of the body, and *kitambi*, a loin cloth similar to hand-woven *kikoi*. Female figures wear *mahando*, a skirt of *kaniki* cloth in white, violet, red or black, and also *kisutu*, the type of *kanga* which has been worn by generations of women at their weddings; worn by the ancestors, *kisutu* encourages wealth and fertility among the women of the house.

sharing in what were once sources of power for these ruling elites that cloth maintains much of its former significance for today's wearers.

From the most elaborate crown to everyday headwear, items to dress and adorn the head are an essential – and ancient – element of clothing throughout Africa. Hats and caps are mainly worn by men, while women often wrap their heads with lengths of cloth or create elaborate hairstyles. Apart from protecting the head from the elements, hats and headdresses are means of identifying personal rank or marital status, as well as religious belief and ethnic and regional affiliation. They are also important personal accessories and, in common with all aspects of clothing today in Africa, they are subject to the scrutiny of the burgeoning contemporary fashion industry. There is probably no better indicator of culture change throughout the world than cloth and clothing, and in Africa the great diversity of textile traditions makes the continent a particularly sensitive barometer for such changes.

Marriage shawl (detail)
Wool, cotton
Sfax, Tunisia, late 20th century
133 x 140 cm
British Museum, Af1997,04.5

The embroidered images of fish, sun and scorpion bring good luck and fertility at the same time as deflecting the Evil Eye. (See p. 149 for full caption.)

Ceremonial skull cap (*chechia*)
Wool, silk
Tunis, Tunisia, 1998 (AH 1418)
11 x 19 cm
British Museum, Af1998,01.123

The red, felted skull cap, *chechia*, is the traditional headwear of Tunisian men. It is created through a complex process that involves knitting, felting, dyeing and brushing. The industry has been thriving since at least the fifteenth century, supplying a range of regional varieties not only within Tunisia, but also across many other countries in the region. Today the industry continues in a number of small workshops in the *Suq des Chechia*s in Tunis, where at least ten different types of cap are produced; for each of these types there will be a range of qualities available. This example is a de luxe version made from Australian merino sheep's wool. It would be worn on ceremonial occasions by important men from Tunis and northern regions of the country. Several different types and colours are made for the Tunisian market, and still more for export.[99] A distinctively shaped version in black with a central stalk is made for the Libyan market and was frequently worn by Colonel Gaddafi.

A craftsman raises the nap on the surface of a *chechia* using an implement made from the head of a giant teasel plant. He wears a leather knee guard (*kukan*) and is sitting on a pile of hinged, wooden presses within each of which is a folded *chechia*. To his right are packages containing completed *chechias*.

Legend has it that an Andalusian girl, fleeing from Christian persecution in the sixteenth century, came as a refugee to northern Tunisia. As she combed her hair the seeds of a teasel plant, which had become entangled there, fell to earth; soon the teasels sprang up and with them the *chechia* industry was born.

Reversible dress (*te eraz*)
Silk, synthetics
Harar, Ethiopia, late 20th century
224 x 118 cm
British Museum, Af2002,06.1

Reversible dress (*te eraz*) of a type worn by women of high status in the ancient walled city of Harar in southern Ethiopia.[100] The darker, more subdued dress might be worn at funerals or at public events where women might encounter foreign visitors to the city. Turned inside out, the more brightly coloured alternative dress might be worn at neighbourhood festivals, women's association meetings and private entertaining. Although for centuries Harar was a remote, forbidden Muslim city closed to European travellers, it had extensive intercontinental trading links with Syria, India and China, particularly in textiles and luxury materials such as silk.

Marriage shawl
Wool, cotton
Sfax, Tunisia, late 20th century
133 x 140 cm
British Museum, Af1997,04.5

This style of marriage shawl is worn by
women from the coastal villages
surrounding the large, industrial town of
Sfax in Tunisia. Different coloured stripes
denote different family groups in the
region, though all the shawls include
embroidered strips along the edge of the
textile, which is worn over the woman's
head. Multicoloured pom-poms and
embroidered images of fish, stars and
scorpions protect the wearer from the Evil
Eye and also bring wealth and fertility to
the bride. These marriage cloths also
include two lines of 'jewels' created by
tie-dyed patterns of henna, the magical
substance with which the bride is tattooed
on the 'night of henna', *lailat al-hinna*,
before her marriage (see p. 47).

Woman's waist cloth (details)
Raffia
Dida people, Ivory Coast, mid 20th century
40 x 99 cm
British Museum, Af1963,13.37

This resist-dyed, tubular raffia waist cloth would be worn by women from noble families among the Dida people of Ivory Coast, West Africa. These cloths are created using weaving techniques similar to those used to create bags of a similar shape in neighbouring Liberia. In 1990 an elderly woman named Blah, considered by the community to be the most skilful in creating these cloths, described them as the most prestigious garment which could be displayed at local ceremonies: 'It is by this cloth that one recognizes that you descend from an old, rich family rather than being a newly rich person.'[101]

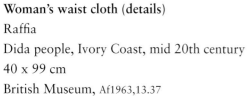

Detail of embroidered panel on the reverse of the dress.

Wedding dress
Cotton, silk, metal
Dakhla Oasis, Egypt, late 20th century
126 x 144 cm
British Museum, Af1991,23.21

This embroidered wedding dress would have been worn by a woman of very high status in the oasis of Dakhla in the Western Desert of Egypt. Dresses of this type are first worn during a woman's wedding and thereafter on special occasions and ceremonies. Each oasis in the Western Desert boasts a different design of dress, and within the larger oases inhabitants of different villages could be distinguished by variations on these designs.[102] This dress was probably embroidered in the village of Qalamun. It has a squared bodice, which is common to all Dakhla dresses, but its pointed, central panel is formed from as many as six separate lines of embroidery, one inside the other, emphasized by several rows of coins.

152

Patterned cloth (*lamba akotofahana*)
Silk
Merina people, Madagascar,
late 19th century
147 x 225 cm
British Museum, Af1969,14.1

The wearing of patterned silk cloth, *lamba akotofahana*, became a mark of status among the aristocracy of the Merina people of pre-colonial Madagascar. Most of the pattern motifs on these cloths, some of them derived from trees and flowers, were named elements which in turn relate to the system of honours that helped to define the complex hierarchy of the Merina kingdom during the nineteenth century. The Malagasy word *manamboninahitra* means 'to hold honours', though its literal translation is 'he who has the flower of grass'.

Cut-pile embroidered cloth
Raffia
Kuba-Shoowa people, Democratic Republic of Congo, early 20th century
50 x 131 cm
British Museum, Af1979,01.2674

Luxurious cut-pile raffia cloths such as this are primarily associated with the funerals of
powerful men – especially court funerals – when they are publically displayed as grave goods
among the Kuba people of the Democratic Republic of Congo. The cloths are painstakingly
embroidered by women, who by implication have neglected other domestic chores to
complete them, and remain unused until the funerary ceremony. The full extent of the
wealth, and thus the social status, of the owner of these cloths is not revealed until his death.

The textile is dyed using natural substances: red from barwood (similar to camwood), yellow from the brimstone tree and black from river mud or charcoal. The textile includes a variety of different patterns and motifs, all of which are named and have particular significance. The supreme importance to the Kuba of pattern, as applied to a wide range of objects, including textiles, is highlighted by the scholar Jan Vansina in the following story (Vansina, J., 1978, *The Children of Woot: A History of the Kuba Peoples*, University of Wisconsin Press, Madison, p. 221): In the 1920s a motorbike was acquired by missionaries working in the Kasai area, and they duly showed it to the Kuba king. To their surprise, the aspect of the bike which most impressed the king was the patterned tracks left by the tread in its tyres. The king ordered that the patterns be copied and entered into the repertoire of Kuba artistry.

Nobleman's cape (*lemd*)
Velvet, silk, metal
Ethiopia, early 20th century
98 x 123 cm
British Museum, Af1974,11.10,
dontated by H. L. Littler

Noblemen's capes, *lemd*, of the late
nineteenth- and early twentieth-century
Ethiopian Empire developed from the form
of earlier honorific lion-skin capes. The
pendant panels represent, in stylized form,
the limbs and paws of the lion. Luxury
imported materials such as velvet, silk,
gold and silver were usually included in
these prestigious garments.

Some of the elaborate ceremonial dress worn in the past by political and military office holders survive in the robes worn by ecclesiastical officials of the Ethiopian church around the world, particularly at important events in the church calendar such as *Temqat* (Epiphany), here celebrated in London, UK, 2010.

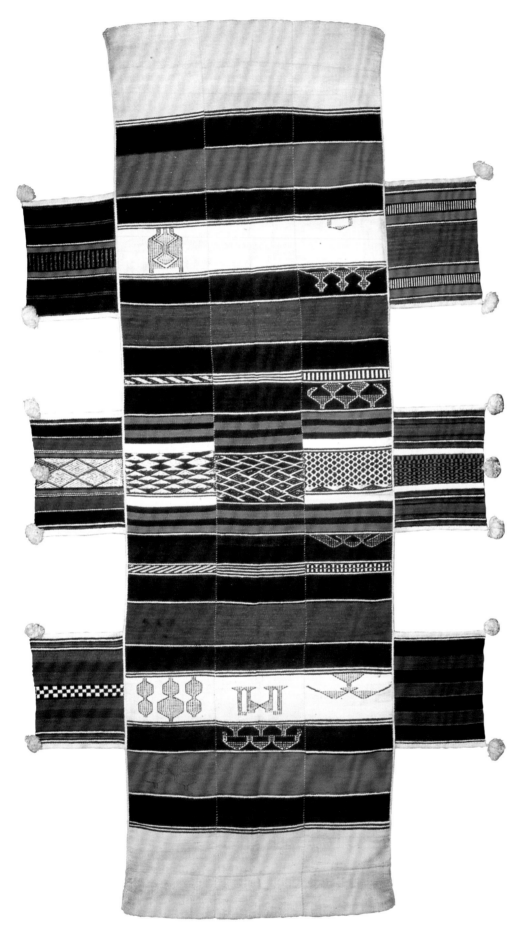

Hammock of narrow-strip cloth
Cotton
Vai people, Sierra Leone,
early 20th century
21 x 122 cm
British Museum, Af1934,0307.183,
donated by Charles A. Beving

Specialist weavers among the Mende and
Vai people of Sierra Leone create broad
strips of cotton cloth, which are sewn
together to create fine textiles, *kpoikpoi*,
with complex tapestry weave patterns. These
textiles are often commissioned for display
at important ceremonial events, though
sometimes a weaver might be approached
to create a fine hammock such as this one,
created by a Vai weaver for use by a chief
as a prestigious means of transport.[103]

Crocheted hat
Wool, cotton, raffia
Cameroon, mid 20th century
15 x 18 cm
British Museum, Af1979,01.4566

Men in the Cameroon Grasslands wear a variety of headgear for both everyday and ceremonial use, in both cases indicating the rank or status of the wearer. These hats are crocheted by men using wool and cotton yarn, often stiffened with raffia fibre, and are thought to represent elaborate hairstyles of the past, or to imitate certain types of Islamic headgear from the Muslim north.[104]

Wax-print cloth

Cotton
Netherlands/Ghana, late 20th century
120 x 184 cm
British Museum, 2011,2002.85

A modern 'wax' print manufactured for
the West African trade by Vlisco in the
Dutch town of Helmond. It incorporates
in a single cloth several versions of very
early popular designs, including the fingers
and hands (though without the coins)
(see pp. 120–21), the *adinkra* symbol
dwennimmen or 'ram's horns', indicating
both humility and strength, and the
umbrella which is an important status
symbol in Ghana (see opposite).

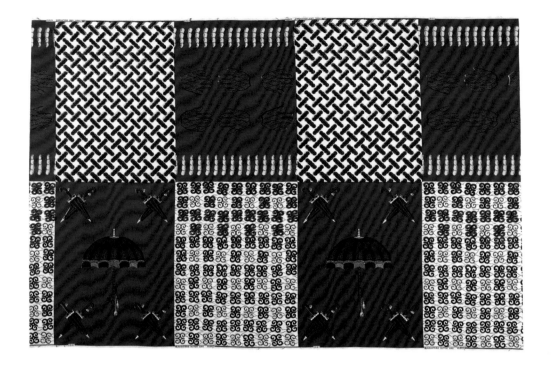

Ceremonial umbrellas displayed during a public appearance by the *Asantehene* (king) in Kumase, Ghana. Imported cloths are usually used in the construction of these umbrellas, but the most prestigious examples often use the richly patterned *arkilla kerka* woollen cloths woven by the Fulbe of Mali (see p. 174).

This nineteenth-century illustration from *Mission from Cape Coast Castle to Ashantee* by Thomas Bowdich, shows the *Asantehene* in procession with many ceremonial umbrellas, *kyinie*. In the nineteenth century there was a village of umbrella makers outside Kumase. Each major state in the Asante kingdom would have had its own umbrella makers, and the umbrella remains an important part of regalia today. Umbrellas perform the physical task of shading the king or chief and of indicating his presence in a crowded parade, but they also create a symbolic space in which a condition of spiritual peace and coolness, *dwo*, exists.[105]

Colour symbolism in textiles

Zulu Zionists near Laduma's homestead, South Africa, in 1977. The colour symbolism of their garments probably relates to the Zulu associations of white as representing spiritual purity, red and black as death and sin, and blue as a mediator between the two.

The *mganga* (spirit healer) Bibi Akili Ubwani (pseudonym) and her assistants following an exorcism of a man, possessed by spirits through witchcraft, near the town of Bagamoyo, Tanzania in 2002. The Bibi (right) wears a style, pattern and colour of *kanga* which I have never seen since, specially imported from the Masood Textile Mills in Faisalabad, Pakistan, and undoubtedly signifying her status as an *mganga* with extraordinary powers, as well as her position as leader. The group had been requested to come to Bagamoyo from the southern province of Mtwara because the local *mganga* was not powerful enough to deal with an 'outbreak' of witchcraft in the town. Her assistants wore distinctive red and black, military style 'uniforms' which communicate a powerful message to the evil spirits which they struggle to overcome. In answer to why her assistants wear red, white and black clothing, the Bibi replied: 'Red and white are the colours of the *mganga*; black was used by our ancestors when they were performing this profession – they had no access to other colours – and so some of us wear black out of respect for and in memory of them'.[106]

PATTERNS OF THOUGHT: TEXTILES AND SYSTEMS OF BELIEF IN NORTH AND WEST AFRICA

Embroidered wedding dress (*asherah nahuak*) (detail)
Silk, synthetics, shell
Siwa Oasis, Egypt, late 20th century
115 x 180 cm
British Museum, Af1991,11.1

This embroidered wedding dress, *asherah nahuak*, is made of silk and synthetic material to which various charms, such as pearl buttons, hands, horns and horseshoes, have been attached to ward off the Evil Eye and bring good fortune. The 'white dress' is worn on the third day of the Siwan bride's wedding celebrations, when she receives her parents and family for the first time in her new home. The red, green and orange embroidery is said to represent the colours of ripening dates. Throughout North Africa dates are offered or received by wedding participants in an attempt to ensure the fertility of bride and groom. In Siwa, dates are a major cash crop and also signify wealth and economic stability. Conversely, the red, yellow and orange threads may suggest the colours of the sun – Siwa has a well-documented link with the ancient Egyptian sun god Amun-Re.

Patterns of thought: textiles and systems of belief in North and West Africa

Allah bar Sarki

'Allah spare the King'

HAUSA EMBROIDERY PATTERN NAME, NORTHERN NIGERIA[107]

The peoples living in the lands surrounding the Sahara Desert are broadly united by a single common element in their allegiance to Islam, despite their ethnic and cultural diversity. In one way or another, this religious affiliation shapes and informs the arts and cultures of the region, and nowhere is this more evident than in the textile arts. However, it is important to remember that Islam, far from annihilating earlier cultures and beliefs, instead adapted to and assimilated them, often resulting in syncretic religious beliefs which in turn are reflected by the extraordinarily rich and diverse textile traditions of the region.

In the seventh century AD Muslim armies invaded North Africa and began the process which, despite resistance from the indigenous Imazighen (Berber) peoples, culminated in the establishment of the Hispano-Mauresque civilization that flourished in the Maghrib countries (Libya, Tunisia, Algeria and Morocco) and southern Spain from the tenth to the fifteenth centuries AD. At about the same time the great Sahelian empires – Ghana, Mali, Songhay and Kanem-Bornu – rose to power in the lands to the south of the Sahara, their dominance depending on vast armies of warriors on horseback. Trading networks opened up across the Sahara, and with the caravans came Islamic scholars who helped in the gradual conversion to Islam of these Sahelian empires, linking the great centres of learning in North Africa, such as Kairouan in Tunisia, with the new mosques and universities established at Timbuctu and Jenne in Mali.

Granada in southern Spain fell to Christian armies in 1492, effectively bringing an end to the Hispano-Mauresque civilization and to a fruitful period of cultural and scientific exchange between Islam and Christian Europe. Many Muslim and Jewish artists, including weavers and embroiderers, sought refuge in the large towns of North Africa, and at this point, a particular pattern of production, use of materials, and division of labour was established in the Maghrib, which remains essentially unchanged today. Weaving in towns is carried out by men, using double-heddle looms and often incorporating luxury materials such as silk and metallic threads of gold and silver. In rural regions, weaving is done by women using upright, single-heddle looms, predominantly using wool as the raw material; here the cut and sewn garments of the city tend to be replaced by single-piece draped or wrapped clothes for women, secured by a *fibula*, or cloak pin.

In the regions surrounding the Sahara, as in all Muslim societies, marriage is seen as the ideal adult state. Clothing for both bride and groom reflects their new social status as well as concerns over modesty and fertility; perhaps most importantly, clothing is seen to ease the passage from the unmarried to the married state and the patterning of garments is crucial in facilitating this transition and in guarding against forces, spiritual and physical, which might interrupt or damage this process. Similar patterns are known by different names in different regions of this vast area of the African continent, and do not necessarily have the same significance. However, universal concerns regarding protection from harm, and the promotion of good luck, health, and fertility are preoccupations that inform the patterning of textiles and other artefacts throughout the region, both in rural and urban environments.[108]

A belief in the destructive effects of the Evil Eye is a global phenomenon and was certainly widespread in North Africa before the coming of Islam with the Arab invasions of the seventh century. However, because the Evil Eye is best described as the first covetous glance cast by one person on something belonging to another, the warnings in the Qur'an to beware of the envious person fostered this existing fear and linked it inextricably to Islam. Much of the iconography to be found in the decorative patterning of artefacts in the lands surrounding the Sahara may be directly related to various means of thwarting the Evil Eye, *'ayn al-hasūd*, and inevitably textiles – particularly those which are worn – have received special attention in this respect. Stylized representations of sharp objects such as knives or cloak pins (*fibulae*), reflective objects such as mirrors, sequins, buttons or the eye itself, and 'repulsive' objects such as scorpions, snakes and bones are applied to the design of textiles in various ways to pierce, reflect or repel the Evil Eye.[109] These motifs, together with a host of others intended to bring wealth, health and fertility, combine to make the patterning of textiles in the region intensely complex and spiritually significant.

The number five, *khamsa*, is particularly beneficial and occurs in a number of patterns, though when reproduced in the form of an open hand it combines many of the concerns represented in the other symbols so far discussed. It has the ability to pierce the Evil Eye with its straightened fingers – 'there's five in your eye' is a common Arabic insult – but it also refers to Fatima, daughter to Muhammad and the protection she brings. A further connection is to the supplicatory gesture of the Muslim at prayer, and – particularly when included in the patterning of women's garments – to the upraised hands of the bride on the third day of her wedding when she 'presents' herself to her relatives and to those of the groom.

Textiles – in particular men's and women's dress – may relate to supernatural or religious power in many different ways, whether through patterning, the use of particular materials and attachments, or the manner in which – and occasions on which – they are worn or displayed. Throughout the lands surrounding the Sahara in North and West Africa, the force driving the creation of the wonderfully diverse traditions of 'spiritually inspired' textiles in the region has been Islam.

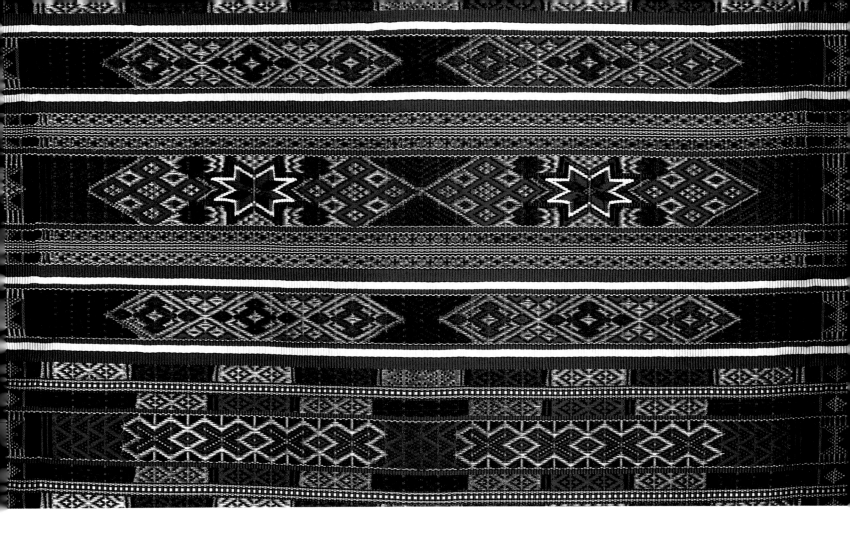

Woman's wrap-around garment (*rida' ahmar*) (detail)
Silk, metallic thread
Atelier of Karim el-Arousse, Mahdia, Tunisia, 1998 (AH 1418)
135 x 466 cm
British Museum, Af1998,01.81

Many types of patterned cloth produced today in North Africa have a long ancestry. The
atelier of Karim el-Arousse of Mahdia, Tunisia wove this wrap-around garment *rida' ahmar*
('red shawl/outer garment') in 1998 (AH 1418).[110] Although the base cloth is black, it is
known as the 'red' shawl because of the colour's association with marriage and fertility. It is
the most prestigious of all Mahdia's textiles. The patterns of *rida' ahmar* can be traced back
to the Hispano-Mauresque civilization of the tenth to fifteenth centuries. Coloured silk and
metal threads, in individual shuttles, are worked by hand to form named design bands at
either end of the cloth. The central pattern, *dar-al-wust* ('the house in the middle') includes
stylized representations of the mosque (eight-pointed star), the *imam* (the small gold lozenge
in the middle of the star), the separation of men and women (the pairs of dark blue patterns
on either side of the star) and the five daily prayers of Islam (the five interconnected,
diamond-shaped motifs in red). The Star of David motif, which occurs elsewhere on the
textile, commemorates the Jewish weavers who originally wove this type of cloth in Mahdia.

Above The tomb of a *marabout* (holy man) in Kairouan, Tunisia photographed in the 1930s.

Above right Tent-hangings in a Cairo street.

Right **Appliqué tent-hanging**
Cotton on canvas
Egypt, mid 20th century
260 x 170 cm
British Museum, Af1979,10.1.a, donated by Mrs Margaret Isobel Massey Stewart

Spectacular appliqué textiles are used to create large tents in Egypt's towns and cities to accommodate guests at weddings, funerals or other important ceremonies (see pp. 8–9). Panels are also strung between lamp posts to mark the celebration of a local festival or a *moulid* (saint's day). This tent-hanging combines formal geometric and floral elements with script and figurative images. The central design features opposing lions with human faces chained to the base of a stylized tree. Pairs of lions, often bearing swords, were carved into nineteenth-century Egyptian marriage chests and are seen painted above doorways on the façades of Nubian houses. The inscription at the top of the hanging reads: 'There is no victory except from God'; there are also phrases of greeting and welcome below.

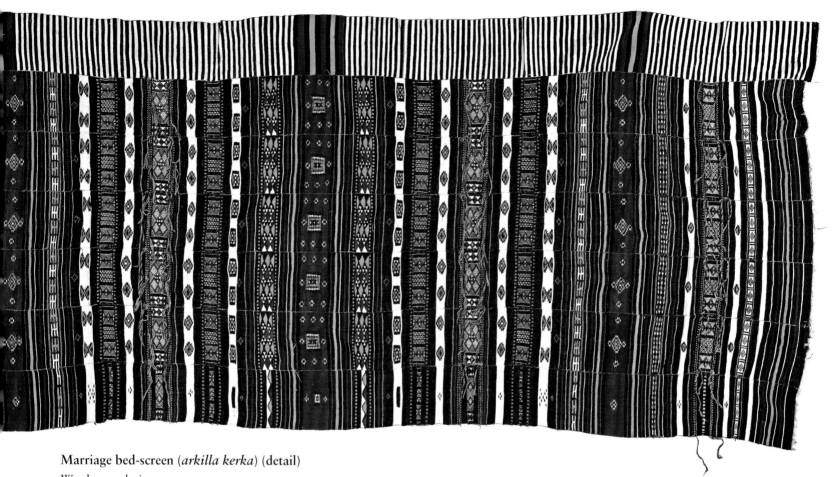

Marriage bed-screen (*arkilla kerka*) (detail)
Wool, goat hair
Fulbe people, Mali, late 20th century
161 x 442 cm
British Museum, Af1986,11.1

The enormous woollen marriage bed-screens used by the Fulbe people in the Inland Delta of the River Niger in Mali are known as *arkilla kerka* and are commissioned by the bride's mother from a male weaver, *maabo*, who belongs to a specialized cast of weavers. The *arkilla kerka* acts as a mosquito net, but its main 'function' may be understood through the names of the various patterns incorporated into its structure, which are designed to confer a mixture of religious blessing combined with cosmic and domestic harmony and fertility. The main motif on the central russet, tapestry-woven band is *lewruwal ye kode*, 'moon and stars'; other named patterns include *almaaje*, 'the leader', *jugal buragi*, 'the tying post for the Prophet Muhammad's horse, Al Burak', *obalaaje*, 'fishing nets' and *tshaldi burgal*, 'milk whisk'. A good quality *arkilla kerka* is always composed of seven strips sewn together. The top strip is used to hang the textile and is known as *sigaretti*, 'cigarettes', composed predominantly of narrow black and white stripes; the bottom strip, *bippol*, touches the bed and is therefore less visible, which may account for the fact that the patterns on this strip are always simpler and smaller versions of those above them.[111] The pattern motifs on this and other types of cloth woven in the Inland Delta are similar to those which may be seen on certain textiles of North Africa, which for centuries had been traded across the Sahara and transferred to the river systems of the Niger on their journey to the coast of West Africa.

War shirt (*batakari*)
Cotton, leather, wool, fur
Asante people, Ghana, early 20th century
97 x 130 cm
British Museum, Af1978,22.310

This war shirt (*batakari*) of the Asante people of Ghana protects its owner through a combination of magical signs and symbols drawn onto the surface of the cloth and protective charms encased in leather pouches attached to the front of the garment. Charm gowns were worn by hunters and soldiers from an early date in Islamic West Africa, particularly among Mande-speaking peoples living in the Sahel on the southerly fringes of the Sahara. The custom spread south to the non-Islamic peoples of the forest kingdoms of West Africa, such as the Asante, where it was recorded by the traveller and diplomat Thomas Bowdich in 1819.[112] There the *batakari*, while maintaining its protective function, was also worn on ceremonial occasions – the *batakari kese* or 'great war shirt' is still worn by paramount chiefs of the Asante.

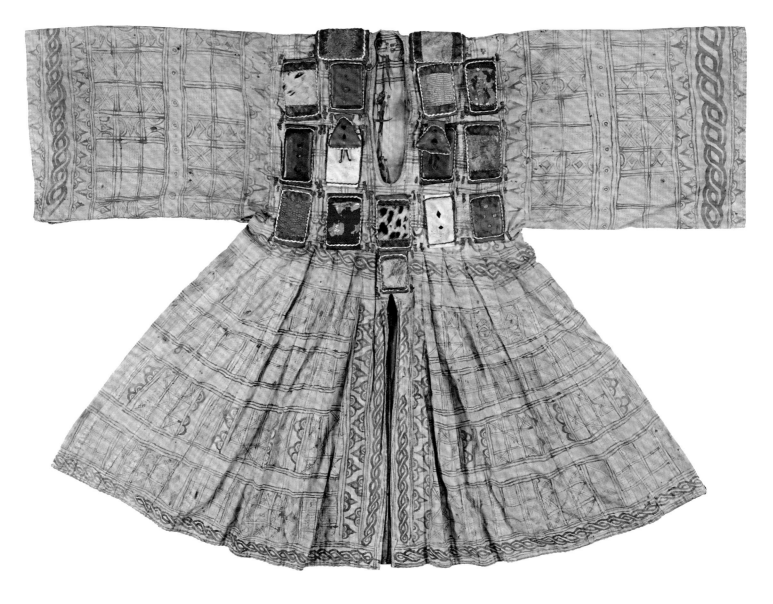

'Big gown' (*babar riga*)
Silk, cotton
Northern Nigeria, early 20th century
128 x 270 cm
British Museum, Af1934,0307.200, donated by Charles A. Beving

The most spectacular garment worn by men of great standing in Hausa, Yoruba and Nupe society in northern Nigeria is the *babar riga*, 'big gown'. It is made of numerous strips (this example has no fewer than 126) of woven cloth, hand-sewn together selvage to selvage – the magenta silk used in these woven strips is traded across the Sahara, probably from Tunisia. These gowns are the products of many hands and of different ethnic groups: [113] the spinner, the weaver, the specialist draughtsman who creates the designs for the embroiderer to recreate, the embroiderer who creates separate sections (known as *linzami* and *aljihu*) which make up the areas around the neck and the large pocket of the gown, and finally the tailor who assembles all the component parts into the completed gown, which is then beaten over a log using wooden mallets to create a glossy, compacted sheen. [114]

Left Detail of the embroidered neck, showing the *aska takwas* 'eight knives' pattern (see p. 178).

Opposite Embroidering a gown, Bouaké, Ivory Coast.

**Design for embroiderer to copy
by Malam Sa'adu**
Brown ink on paper
Hausa people, Kano, Nigeria, 1971
29 x 20 cm
British Museum, 2008,2025.185.f

Among the most common motifs created
by specialist draughtsmen are the
combination of pointed elements known
as *aska takwas*, 'eight knives', the circular
device with concentric rings known as
tambari, 'drum' and the inter-linked *dagi*
or 'knot' – the last two motifs are
combined in this drawing. The eight
knives, arranged around the neck of the
garment, are designed to protect the owner
from the Evil Eye and from any malicious
forces which might enter at this most
vulnerable point.

Printed shirt
Cotton
Manchester, UK/Nigeria, early 20th century
67 x 97 cm
British Museum, Af1934,0307.220, donated by Charles A. Beving

This garment is a factory printed shirt, probably made in Manchester, UK, by Blakeley and Beving Ltd. Charles A. Beving was a textile trader who made a detailed study of West African textile traditions with a view to sourcing likely designs which could be produced in Manchester. Certain Hausa embroidery motifs such as *aska takwas* ('eight knives') have been accurately copied on this shirt but then arranged in a haphazard fashion, unlike the careful placement of design elements on a hand-made gown.

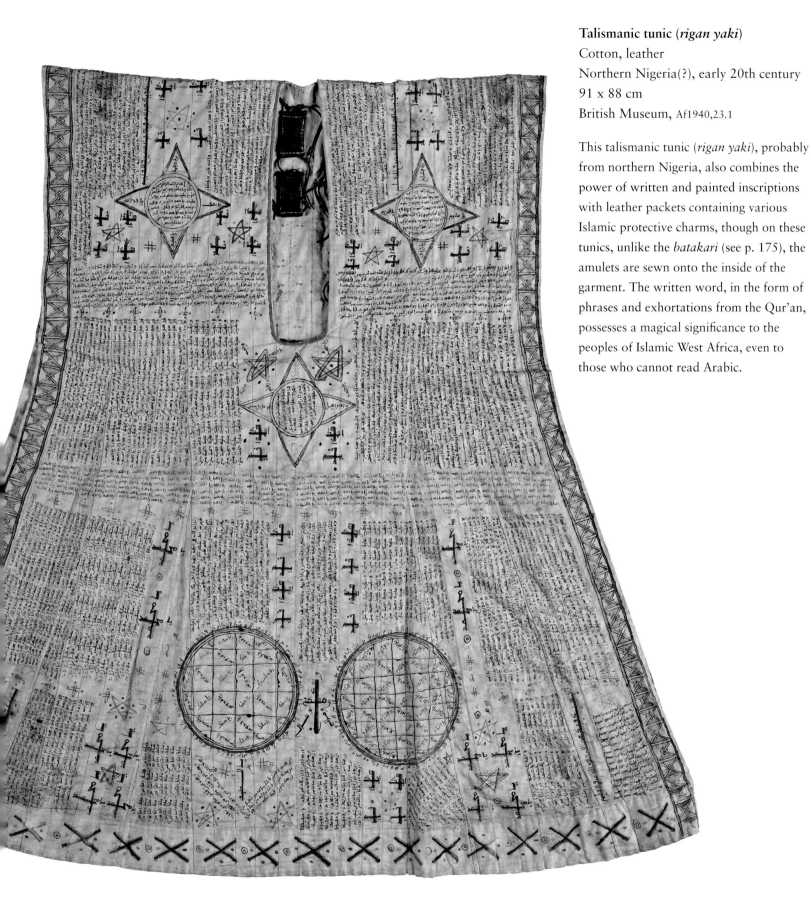

Talismanic tunic (*rigan yaki*)
Cotton, leather
Northern Nigeria(?), early 20th century
91 x 88 cm
British Museum, Af1940,23.1

This talismanic tunic (*rigan yaki*), probably from northern Nigeria, also combines the power of written and painted inscriptions with leather packets containing various Islamic protective charms, though on these tunics, unlike the *batakari* (see p. 175), the amulets are sewn onto the inside of the garment. The written word, in the form of phrases and exhortations from the Qur'an, possesses a magical significance to the peoples of Islamic West Africa, even to those who cannot read Arabic.

Hooded cloak (*akhnif*)
Wool, goat hair
Chleuh Imazighen people, Morocco,
late 19th century
124 x 355 cm
British Museum, Af,+.5773, donated by
Sir Augustus Wollaston Franks

This nineteenth-century hooded cloak
(*akhnif*) of wool and goat hair would have
been worn by a man of the Chleuh
Imazighen (Berber) people of Aït
Ouaouzguite in Morocco. Requiring an
extraordinary degree of technical expertise,
these cloaks were woven to shape by
women to create a semi-circular form on
an upright, single-heddle loom. The
distinctive orange-red 'eye' design on the
back of the garment was believed to
protect against the Evil Eye. It was
elaborated with supplementary weft
patterning, and further motifs were
embroidered by men.[115] Jewish and Chleuh
men and boys wore these cloaks, but adult
Jews were obliged to wear the garment
with the design facing inwards.

These Gnawa musicians from southern Morocco were photographed by the artist Hassan Hajjaj in 2010 (AH 1431). The Gnawa are a distinct ethnic group who trace their origins and some of their belief systems, dress and music to sub-Saharan Africa, although their culture and traditions share some similarities to other groups of Islamic mystics, such as the Sufi brotherhoods. Gnawa musicians and dancers wear costumes and colours which illustrate their diverse heritage – the cowrie-shell hats and other accoutrements have their roots in sub-Saharan Africa, whereas the *djellaba* gowns and black-work embroidery are characteristic of the Maghrib countries of North Africa. Colours have a particular significance in Gnawa ceremonial dress[116] – the man on the right wears a yellow *djellaba* in honour of the powerful female spirits or *Jnun*, belief in which also has its roots in West Africa. However, he also has the Hand of Fatima embroidered on his gown, which will protect him from the *Jnun* should they turn against him.

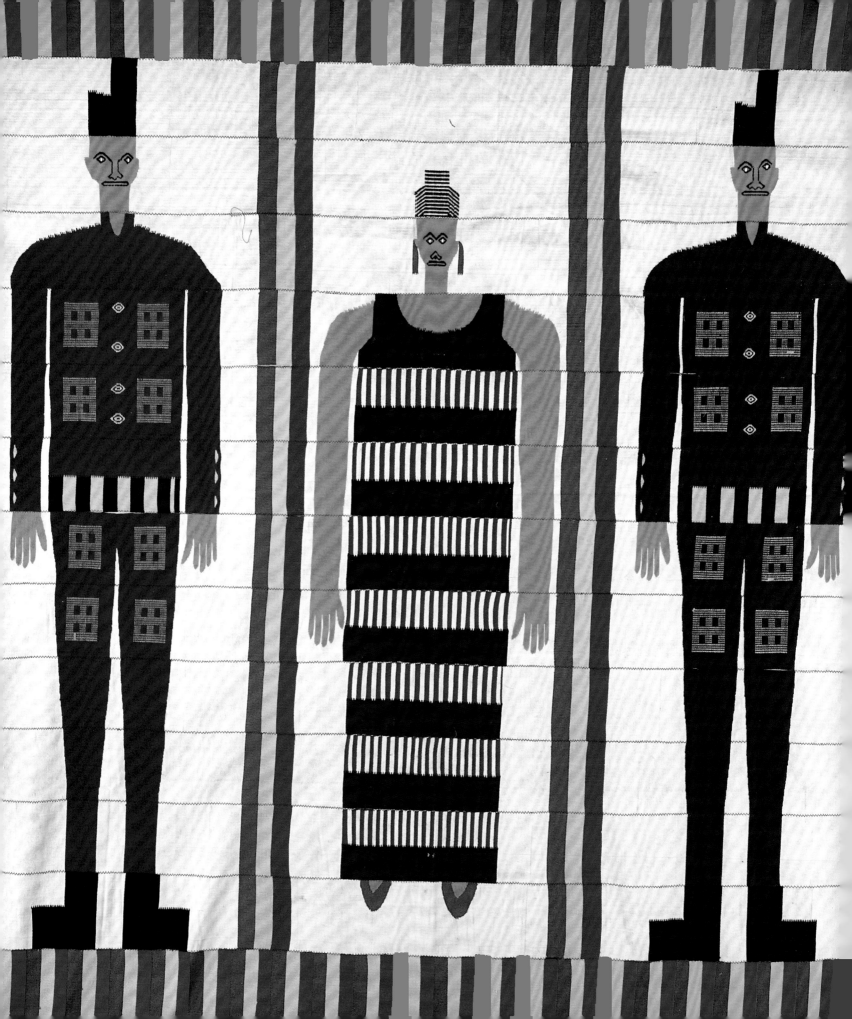

TEXTILES AND COMMUNICATION

Wall-hanging (*couverture personnage*) (**detail**)
woven by Oumar Bocoum
Cotton
Segou, Mali, 1996
180 x 376 cm
British Museum, Af2005,08.1

This detail shows the central group of figures
on a marriage wall-hanging. (See pp. 206–207
for full caption.)

Textiles and communication

Umewacha mlango wazi, paka amekula andazi,
una shauri gani mpangaji
'You left the door open, so the cat ate the doughnut;
what are you going to do about it, tenant?'
INSCRIPTION ON *KANGA* CLOTH FROM ZANZIBAR

We might take a guess at what the 'door', the 'cat' and the 'doughnut' might signify in this veritable novella of a *kanga* inscription; the Swahili woman who wore it in the Zanzibar of the 1960s (and the person or persons to whom it was directed) would have known exactly what was intended. They would also have understood the significance of the Western-style handbag depicted in the centre of the *kanga* – and even the floral pattern running around its border (see p. 190). They might not have been able to read the inscription (in Kiswahili but in the Arabic script) but knowledge of what it meant would have spread rapidly from the vendors, perhaps in Darajani market on Zanzibar, who would have explained it in detail to the women who came to buy the latest 'must-have' design imported from overseas.

Textiles around the world have always offered a means of communicating the most subtle and complex of messages through colour, patterning, materials, inscriptions and the ways in which they are worn or otherwise displayed. However, only on the African continent, with its extraordinary diversity of peoples and cultures, has the practice of communicating through cloth become such a refined and subtle art form. Details of every conceivable facet of life, death and the afterlife may be communicated in one way or another by textiles in Africa. These subjects have been touched on elsewhere in the book, but this chapter will look in more detail at how textiles can communicate or mediate a spectrum of information relating to religious belief and supernatural forces, political affiliation and indoctrination, education and life cycle changes, courtship and marriage, mourning and death.

Religion

The ways in which a person dresses or uses textiles in Africa are very likely to communicate details of his or her religious belief. This is most obvious, of course, in the dress of religious leaders or spirit healers, but also in that of their followers, such as those of the Mahdi and his successor, the Khalifa, in late nineteenth-century Sudan. There, the ragged *muraqqa'a*, which had been the dress of Sufi ascetics for centuries in the Islamic world, was transformed into the *jibba* in a variety of regional styles, versions of which are still worn today[117] (see pp. 42–3). More recently, the followers of Isaiah Shembe in South Africa can instantly be recognized by their dress, the styles of beadwork they wear and even the accoutrements they carry, such as furled umbrellas[118] (see p. 193). Undoubtedly the accessibility of factory-printed cloth, both produced in Africa and imported from overseas, has made it easier for religious leaders to found new organizations and to advertise these through commissioning printed cloth for their followers to wear, as in the case of the many newly formed West African churches such as the Holy Sabbath Mission in Nnobi, eastern Nigeria.

Politics

Textiles in Africa have long been a means of communicating political messages at a local, national and even international level. On a local level, cloth may celebrate the qualities of a particular town, such as Ibadan in Nigeria, or it may be used to reinforce and communicate the powers vested in a secret society, such as Ogboni, the members of which form the judiciary of the Yoruba of Ijebu-Ode, Nigeria. In the post-colonial period, individual politicians and political parties often use cloth as a means of selling themselves to the electorate, and by the same token voters can communicate their political allegiance by the textiles they wear, or the way in which they wear them. However, the printed portrait on a textile may work against the politician concerned, as it enables African voters to show their disapproval, perhaps by wearing the image upside down in public – and perhaps by sitting on it for good measure.

Education

Textiles are frequently used to communicate knowledge of various kinds, from the collective wisdom of the Dowayo people of Cameroon, imparted to male initiates through 'Fire Cloths',[119] (see p. 196) to a proud proclamation of literacy and numeracy through the 'ABC' design of printed cloths (p. 199), which have been popular in West Africa for well over a century. Health and well-being are inevitably primary concerns throughout Africa, concerns communicated by textiles in a variety of ways, from the message on a Tanzanian *kanga*, 'Don't be boastful ... have you been checked?' (for HIV and AIDS), to the benefits of a settled family life, as depicted on the textiles produced to mark both the International Day of the Family and the fiftieth anniversary of Cameroonian independence on 15 May 2010 (p. 201).

Courtship and marriage

Chapter Six (pp. 140–65) looked at the significance of wedding dresses from various parts of Africa; this chapter will deal with various other types of textiles which are used to communicate a variety of details concerning courtship and marriage. Information about the family group of the bride, particularly in North Africa, may be conveyed by the pattern and colouring of marriage shawls, such as those worn by women in the villages around Sfax in Tunisia. In Mali, a long tradition of making hangings, tent-dividers and bedspreads to celebrate marriage has evolved from intricately patterned textiles to bold, figurative designs in which women are offered the choice between a happy married life, with all its benefits, and the money to be earned by selling their bodies. In eastern Africa, *kangas* proclaim the importance of marriage, but also the importance of the wedding itself as something to be enjoyed by the whole community, bringing people together in a unifying process which is beneficial to all concerned, whatever their religious belief.

Death and the afterlife

No discussion of the communicating power of cloth would be complete without mentioning its widespread use at funerals and during funerary rituals. As the anthropologist Victor Turner pointed out, 'Celebration of the dead in most societies is also the celebration of the survivors',[120] and in Africa textiles frequently play a central role in this process. In many parts of Africa, textiles worn by both men and women to signify their marital and social status may also be the shroud they wear as they pass through to another life. The dark red or blue cloth worn at an Asante funeral in Ghana not only distinguishes the close relations of the deceased from the extended family and friends, but also serves to bring them together as a unified group, albeit within an accepted hierarchy. Among the Kuba people of the Democratic Republic of Congo, a man's true status in life may only be communicated after his death by the display and quality of the cut-pile cloth he has accumulated throughout his life. Among some African peoples, a way of overcoming the inevitable disruption to the community at the death of a wealthy or high-ranking man or woman is by passing on inherited collections of cloth to close relations. Certain garments will be worn by relatives on important occasions in the future, and thus the deceased will live on in the community in a very special way.

I recently wore my grandfather's dinner jacket and trousers to a gala event to celebrate the launch of the South African Mapungubwe Golden Rhino Film Festival; my son also wore that dinner jacket on another occasion (lucky we are/were all roughly the same size!) and we both felt a strong sense of continuity and inherited values. In Africa the passing on of inherited dress and other textiles assists in the re-establishment of the essential structure of society and the strengthening of ties among the living, both with one another and with the ancestors.

Printed cloth (*kanga*)
Cotton
Zanzibar, Tanzania, 1960s
108 x 153 cm
British Museum, Af2003,21.1

This *kanga* from Zanzibar, probably dating to the 1960s, shows an open Western-style handbag with metal clasp. The inscription, in Kiswahili written in the Arabic script, reads: You left the door open, so the cat ate the doughnut; what are you going to do about it, tenant? According to *kanga* lore, in Kenya at least, the inscriptions were introduced by Kaderdina Haji Essak, whose initials K. H. E. are still printed on *kangas* produced by the firm he founded in 1887, Mali Ya Abdulla of Biashara Street, Mombasa. The early *kanga* inscriptions, though in Kiswahili, were printed in Arabic script. Kiswahili was latinized in the mid-1900s, and after the First World War Kaderdina's inscriptions began to appear in this lettering, though I suspect this practice did not become widespread until the 1960s when a large proportion of the population had learned to read the latinized script. Today some *kangas* printed for the women of Zanzibar, Oman and Yemen still have inscriptions in the Arabic script.

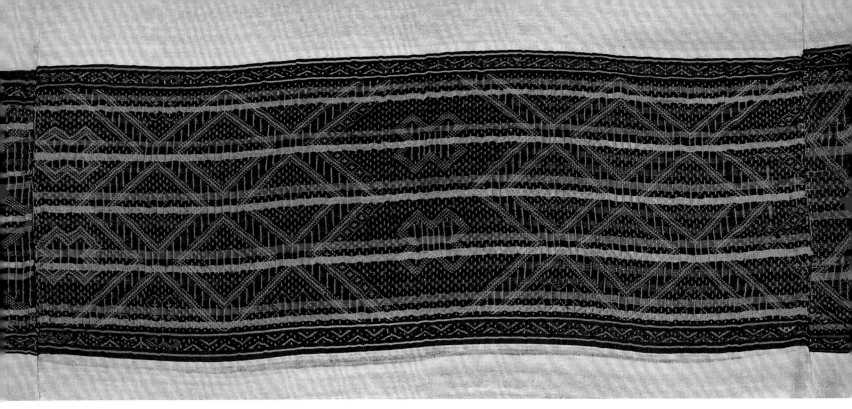

Shawl (*shamma*) (detail)
Cotton, silk
Ethiopia, mid 20th century
149 x 235 cm
British Museum, Af1974,11.5,
donated by H. L. Littler

In Ethiopia, cotton shawls, *shamma*, at
one time minutely defined the social
position of the wearer. A multicoloured
and elaborately patterned silk band, *tibeb*,
woven into the *shamma*, became more
widely worn by the elite of Orthodox
Christian society in the central and
northern highlands of Ethiopia during the
late nineteenth century, replacing a type
with a single red band which had been
fashionable wear for well-to-do men and
women up until that time.[121] These
prestigious shawls, in common with
textiles such as the *lamba akotofahana*
of Madagascar, were ultimately used as
shrouds for the dead. Today the *tibeb* is
woven in rayon, in a wide variety of
designs, and it may be worn by a still
wider cross section of society.

A mid-nineteenth century illustration
showing a type of *shamma* with a red
border being worn by an Ethiopian
courtier (left) and a church lawyer. The
way in which the *shamma* is draped can
communicate the mood and attitude of the
wearer. The courtier is showing deference
to a superior, whereas the lawyer is
walking, in relaxed mood, in the street.[122]

Fancy-printed cloth

Cotton
Nigeria, early 21st century
184 x 116 cm
British Museum, 2011,2002.11

Based in the town of Nnobi in eastern
Nigeria, the Holy Sabbath of Christ the
King Mission World Wide was established
in AD 2000 by Bishop Michael Nwaobi
Amakaeze, also known as Musa (Moses).
This textile was collected in 2007 in
Cameroon and acted as an effective
method of advertising the movement
through depiction of its leader and the
modern church building.

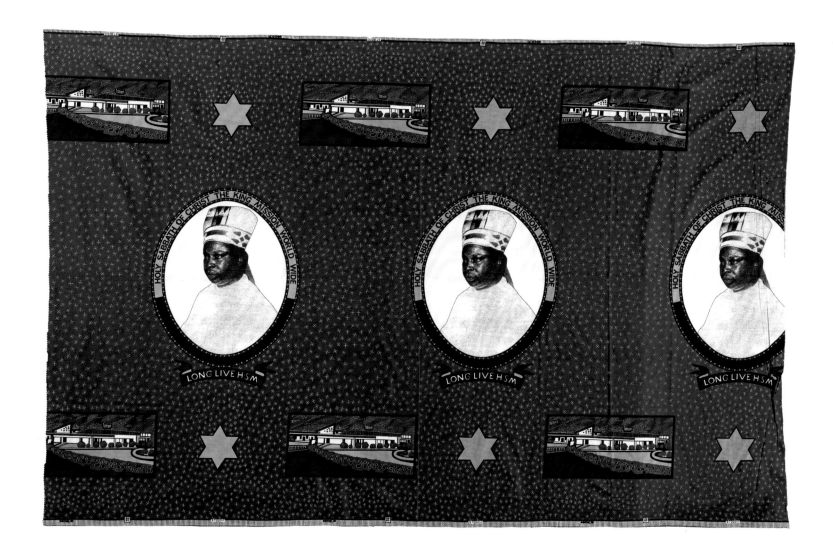

A shrine prepared by nuns in the Benedictine Monastery of the Good News founded in Bouaké, Ivory Coast, in 1962. The shrine is draped with a prestigious indigo resist-dyed cloth, upon which an image of Michael the Archangel has been laid; interestingly enough, the image is a reproduction of a fifteenth-century icon in the Archangel Cathedral of the Moscow Kremlin. At the foot of the shrine stands a typical royal stool of the Baulé people, upon which a lighted candle burns. The shrine communicates a wonderful mixture of African and European images of the divine.

A Zulu woman of South Africa wearing the distinctive beaded costume and furled umbrella that distinguishes her as a follower of the messianic church of Isaiah Shembe (see pp. 241–2).

Printed cloth (*kanga*)
Cotton
Mombasa, Kenya, early 21st century
168 x 107 cm
British Museum, Af2003,21.2

This *kanga* was designed in Mombasa, Kenya, by a member of the Kaderdina family before being sent to India for printing, after which it was returned to Mombasa for sale in 2002. The *kanga* bears an inscription in Kiswahili, SINA SIRI NINA JIBU, which translates as, 'I have no secrets but I have an answer' and was commissioned by the politician Nasir Najib who was seeking election at the time. His name is concealed in the slogan with which he was campaigning.

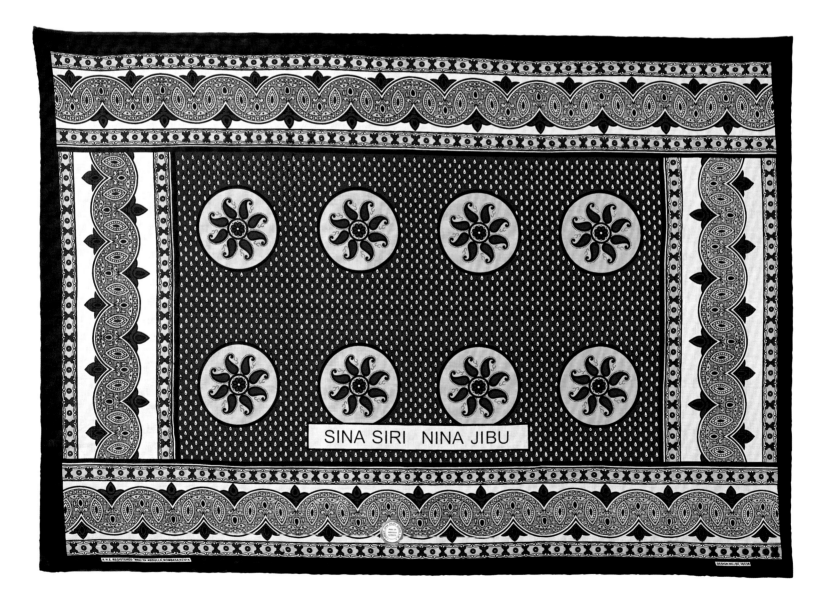

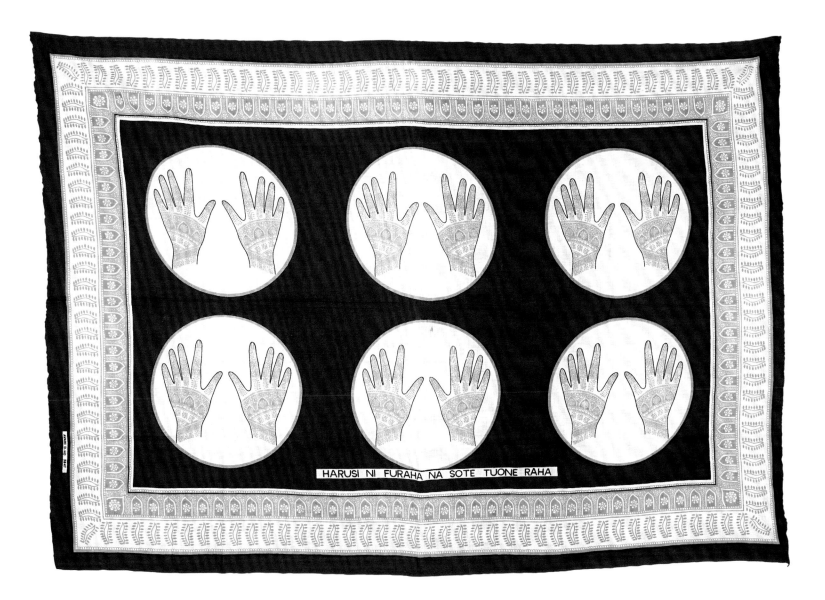

Printed cloth (*kanga*)
Cotton
Tanzania, early 21st century
108 x 156 cm
British Museum, Af2002,09.9

The Kiswahili inscription on this textile reads HARUSI NI FURAHA NA SOTE TUONE
RAHA, 'A wedding is a joyous occasion to be enjoyed by all'. The design includes six pairs
of hands tattooed with henna, a custom common to both Muslim and Hindu brides, and
was calculated to appeal as much to the large Indian diaspora population in eastern Africa
as to the Muslim community. In Islam, henna is viewed as both purifying and protective; it
is thought to be imbued with *baraka* (blessings) and its reddish colour is closely associated
with blood and fertility. In Hindu ritual the application of henna patterns to the hands and
feet is thought to awaken the Inner Light of the bride; it is also applied at important
festivals such as Diwali.

Resist-dyed and appliqué narrow-strip textile or 'Fire Cloth' (*gbanlayo*)
Cotton, felt
Dowayo people, Cameroon, late 20th century
105 x 210 cm
British Museum, Af1984,02.1

'Fire Cloths', *gbanlayo*, are used by the Dowayo people of northern Cameroon during male initiation ceremonies and at the funerary rites of rich men.[123] Alternating appliqué representations of agama lizards and strips of cowrie shells make up the main pattern of the cloth. The cowrie shells represent wealth, whereas the agama lizards, whose heads are reputed to turn bright red with the rising of the sun, serve to 'heat' the cloth, which is wrapped around the young initiate's head. This process 'hardens' the initiate's head as if it were a pot being baked, and as the circumcision takes place, the wisdom of adulthood and of the Dowayo people is imparted. Few 'Fire Cloths' exist in Dowayo society, all of them being owned by rich men who lend them out to initiation ceremonies and funerals. The network of bonds that is established by this process of lending and borrowing is an essential cohesive element in Dowayo social structure.

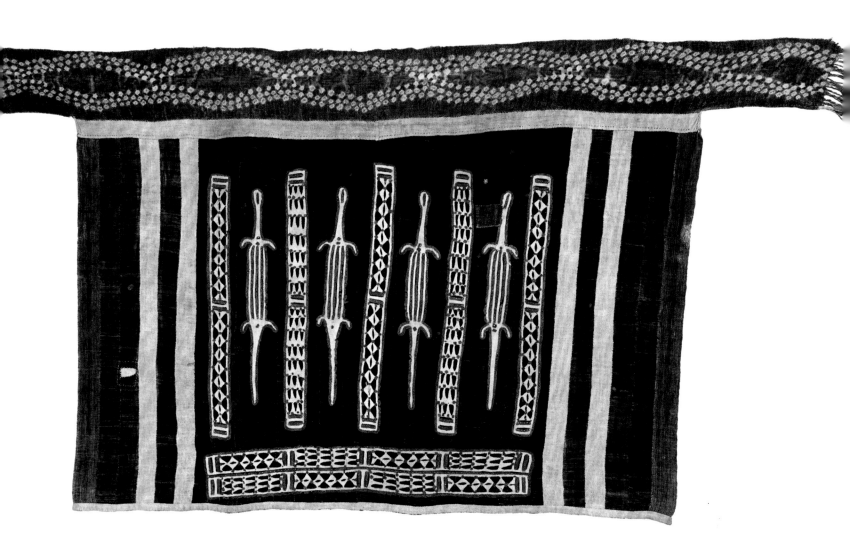

Narrow-strip textile (*aso olona*)
Cotton
Ijebu Yoruba people, Nigeria, mid 20th century
164 x 231 cm
British Museum, Af1966,01.26

Beginning in the late eighteenth century, cloths, *aso olona*, of this pattern became part of
a trading complex with the eastern Ijo people of the Niger Delta, including the Kalabari,
revolving around palm oil. Traditionally woven for members of the Ijebu Yoruba Ogboni
secret society, their popularity with Eastern Ijo peoples derived mainly from the inclusion of
the stylized representations of *ikaki* (tortoise) in the weft-float patterns of these cloths. To
the Kalabari, *ikaki* is a divine being, part trickster, part sage, who, like the tortoise, is able
to withdraw into the world of secrets, good and evil, hidden beneath his shell.[124] In the
nineteenth century the Igbo people of Akwete village (see p. 134) became heavily involved
in the palm oil trade with the Eastern Ijo, and it was at this time that Akwete weavers,
noting the importance to the Eastern Ijo of the Yoruba cloths with *ikaki* patterning, began
to weave cloths of a similar pattern to trade with the Kalabari and other peoples of the
Delta. Gradually the weavers of Akwete superseded the Ijebu Yoruba as the main suppliers
of cloth on commission from Eastern Ijo clients, a situation which remains today.

Embroidered bark-cloth, *Ekigaji* **('Aloe Vera') by Proscovia Nabwami**
Fig tree bark
Kampala, Uganda, 2008
100 x 120 cm
British Museum, 2008,2021.4

This embroidered bark-cloth is titled *Ekigaji* ('Aloe Vera') and was made by Proscovia Nabwami of the Nalumunye Women's Group, Kampala, Uganda in 2008. This work celebrates the many beneficial uses of the aloe vera plant. It was created through the Design, Health and Community project, a collaboration between Northumbria University, UK, Durban University of Technology, South Africa and Makerere University, Uganda. Women from different craft groups in Uganda explore the ancient tradition of bark-cloth making to communicate contemporary concerns, particularly over HIV and AIDS.

Wax-printed cloth
Cotton
Netherlands/West Africa, late 20th century
113 x 181 cm
British Museum, 2011,2002.29

One of the most popular designs of wax-printed cloths, originally created in Europe for the
West African market, is 'ABC', the alphabet cloth. It has been through many permutations
of design, though it usually features the English alphabet presented in a grid of six by six
squares and with a pattern of discs making up the ten additional squares not filled by
individual letters. Such cloths were worn to communicate the literacy of the wearer and also
numeracy if, as in this example, numbers and measurements were included in the design.

***Banks of the Nile*, tapestry by
Sayed Mahmoud**
Wool
Harrania, near Cairo, Egypt, 2008–9
320 x 183 cm
British Museum, 2009,2032.1

This tapestry, entitled *Banks of the Nile*,
was woven over a period of eleven months
(March 2008–February 2009) by Sayed
Mahmoud of the Ramses Wissa Wassef
Arts Centre. The Centre was set up in
1951 by Ramses and his wife Sophie with
the aim of allowing children to express
themselves through the medium of weaving
without using any preliminary sketches,
thus freeing the imagination. Ramses
described the process as follows:

*This is a very slow task, rather like the
generation of living tissues. I attached a
great importance to this slowness, and to
the child's ideas ripening in his mind and
guiding his fingers as they materialised. I
also counted on experience, gained
gradually day by day, giving birth
continually to new images.*[125]

Many of the original group of fourteen
children are still actively weaving, and they
have been joined over the years by second
and third generations of weavers.

Fancy-printed cloth
Cotton
Cameroon, 2007
114 x 181 cm
British Museum, 2011,2002.16

The importance of a stable and happy family life is portrayed in this textile printed for the International Day of the Family in 2007. In 2010 this day coincided with the fiftieth anniversary of Cameroonian independence and reunification, an occasion marked by the simultaneous marriage of 158 couples in the town of Nkoteng.

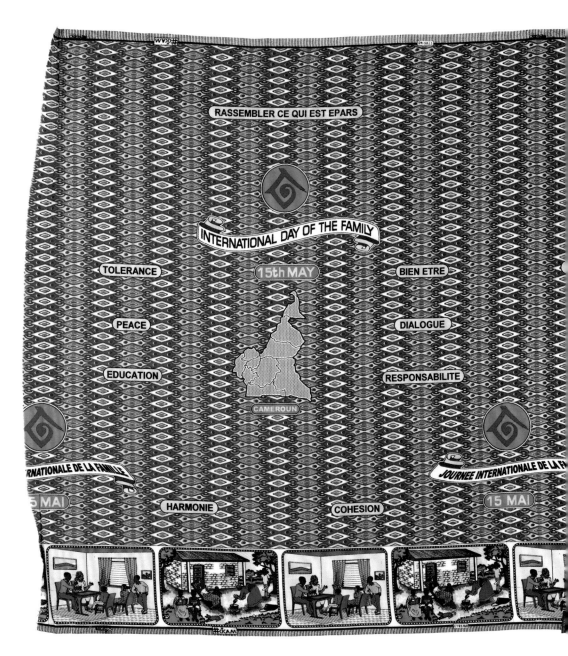

Until quite recently weaving *kente* cloth on the treadle loom was very much a male preserve, but today more and more female weavers are learning the profession. This weaver, from the Volta region of Ghana, wears printed cloth with the repeating motif of a computer to emphasize her modernity.

REAL DIMATEX
100% COTTON 118.50 CM X 10.98 MTS

DIMATEX

GUARANTEED WAX MADE AS HOLL

GUARANTEED DIMATEX

Wax-printed cloth (detail)
Cotton
China/Senegal, 2006
117 x 500 cm
British Museum, Af2006,09.7

In 2006, textiles with the 'gel capsule' pattern were all the rage in Senegal. This example was one of many colours available at HLM market in Dakar, Senegal (see p. 137) and was probably printed in China. The design confers an element of protection and may be understood as part of the great variety of patterns and amulets which, when attached to different forms of dress in Africa, contribute towards the wearer's well-being.

Wax-printed cloth

Cotton

Netherlands/West Africa, late 20th century

111 x 178 cm

British Museum, 2011,2002.32

The electric fan depicted on this textile symbolizes wealth and well-being. 'Who has the means to acquire one?' asks the collector and academic Wolfgang Bender in his notes on this textile, '... and besides that, who has the electricity to run it?'[126] A hugely popular dance in Gambia and Senegal is called *ventilateur*, 'electric fan', and is performed by young women to music known as *Mbalax*, a fusion of traditional Senegambia sounds with western Latin, jazz, soul and rock. The name of the dance derives from the gyrating buttocks of the dancers – a woman wearing this cloth would undoubtedly be reminding admirers of the suggestive movements of the *ventilateur*.

Wax-printed cloth (detail)
Cotton
Netherlands/Democratic Republic of Congo, late 20th century
118 x 153 cm
British Museum, 2011,2002.86

This cloth was first printed in 1940, the date inscribed on each of the six spark plugs (*bougies*) in the design, which references the six-cylinder engines of the most expensive cars available in what was then the Belgian Congo – cars driven in the main by rich foreigners. The phrase 'six spark plugs' had become shorthand to describe the most beautiful women in Congolese society, one of whom is featured in the centre of the design, and as Wolfgang Bender points out, the spark plugs have decidedly phallic connotations.[127] In 2011 the Dutch textile company Vlisco produced a version with eight spark plugs, in homage to the V8 motor, though the central image has been replaced by a *Sapeur*, one of a group of men in Kinshasa and Brazzaville renowned for dressing up in outrageous suits, bowler hats and other accessories – and for smoking large cigars or ornate tobacco pipes. [128]

Marriage wall-hanging (*couverture personnage*) by Oumar Bocoum
Cotton
Segou, Mali, 1996
180 x 376 cm
British Museum, Af2005,08.1

This marriage wall-hanging was woven in 1996 by Oumar Bocoum, a *maabo* (member of a caste specializing in weaving) from the city of Segou in Mali. Textiles such as this are known as *couvertures personnages* and have evolved from the *tapi* or large colourful blankets first woven by a *maabo* named Gwòòtal Bambara in the 1960s. He in turn was succeeded by Abdurrahman Bura Bocoum, who elaborated on his predecessor's innovation by including images of human beings, particularly after the military coup of 1968, when he began to weave soldiers in uniform into his textiles. Oumar Bocoum was a follower of Abdurrahman and represents a third generation of innovative weavers engaged in producing these wall-hangings or bedcovers.[129] This particular example shows a woman standing in the middle of a group of six soldiers. The words woven around the edge of the textile communicate the choice she is presented with: the blessings of marriage, in the form of faithfulness, love, peace, happiness, companionship and longevity; or, 75,000 Malian francs (about £75), the sum she will receive by selling her body to the soldiers.

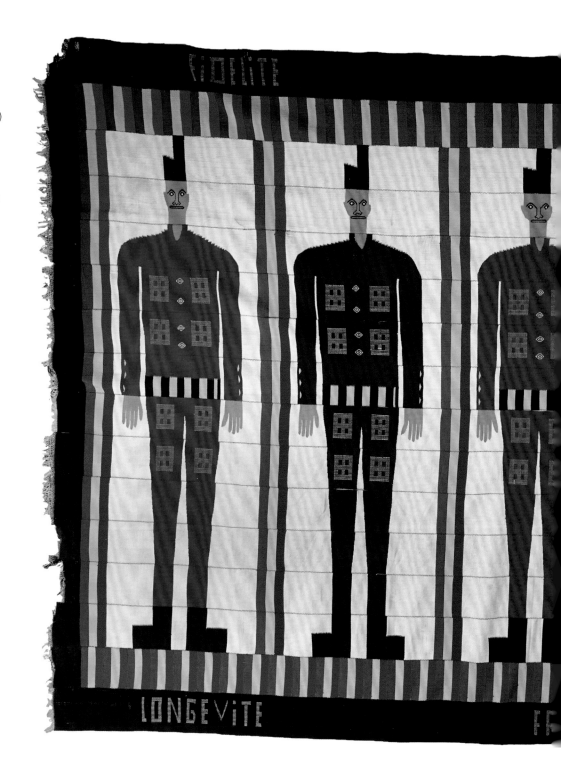

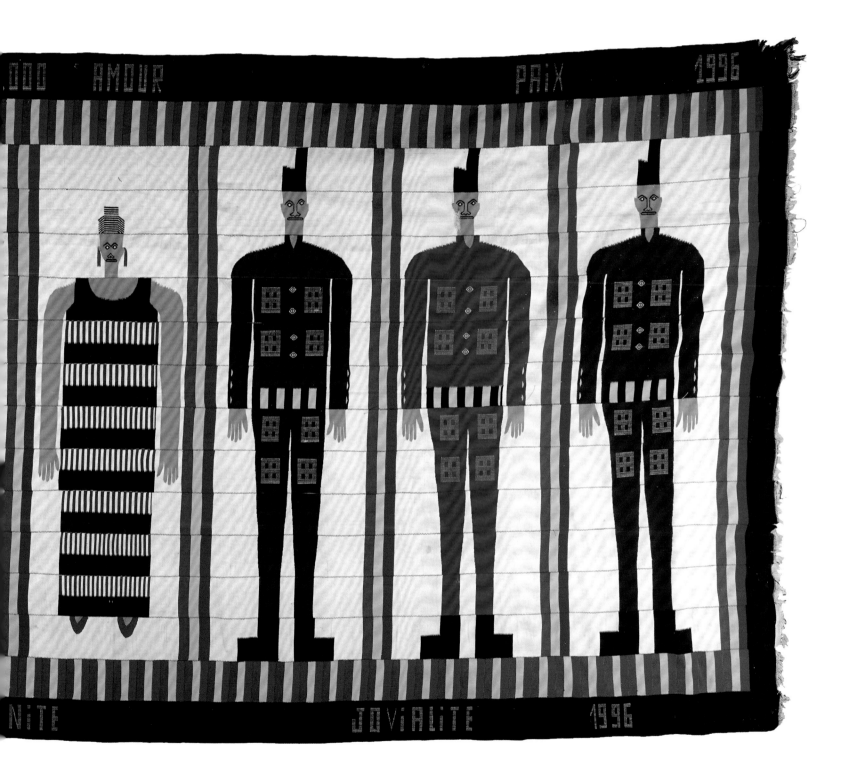

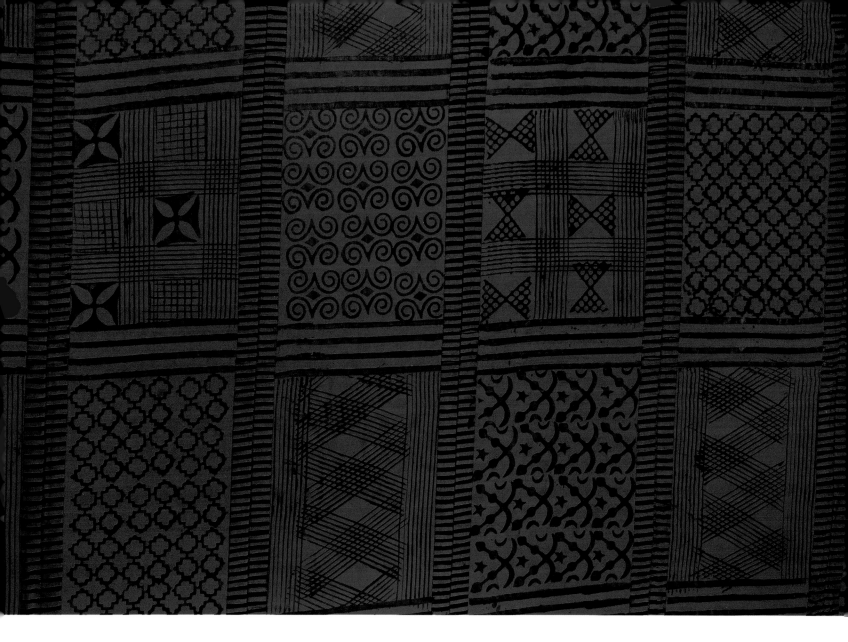

Adinkra mourning cloth (detail)
Cotton, silk
Asante people, Ghana, early 21st century
223 x 350 cm
British Museum, 2008,2031.1, donated by Anthony Griffiths

This *adinkra* mourning cloth of the Asante people of Ghana is composed of seven sections
of machine-woven damask cotton textile, divided by six narrow strips of silk with alternating
red and black stripes. *Adinkra* cloths with dark backgrounds, such as blue, black or russet red,
are worn for funerals or other mortuary rites by men and women in Ghana. Various repeating
motifs of the same form occupy different square or rectangular fields in the composition of all
adinkra cloths. This design includes the motif of crossed swords, *akofena*, denoting courage,
the Maltese cross, *mmusuyidee*, which brings good fortune and sanctity, and the curly ram's
horns, *dwennimmen*, which indicate humility and strength.

Mourning cloth, dark in colour, is worn by Ghanaians at funerals wherever they happen to be in Africa or around the world. Funerals, like weddings and other important events, may also provide an opportunity to be stylish in the appropriate vein. This Ghanaian, wearing mourning cloth, was photographed in Marrakesh, Morocco in 2010 (AH 1431) by the artist Hassan Hajjaj.

THROUGH THE LENS: TEXTILES, ART AND PHOTOGRAPHY IN AFRICA

Les Deux Amies ('The Two Friends')
by Malick Sidibé
Gelatin silver print
Bamako, Mali, 1975

The Malian photographer Malick Sidibé was awarded
the Golden Lion Award for Lifetime Achievement in the
Arts at the fifty-second Venice Biennale in 2007. He was
the first African artist to receive this award in a year
when an African Pavilion also featured in the Biennale
for the first time. Textiles – woven, printed or resist-
dyed – are integral to Sidibé's compositions. He used
the same striped, Malian textile as a backdrop to his
portraits for at least thirty years (see p. 224).

Through the lens: textiles, art and photography in Africa

No medium has been more instrumental in creating a great deal of the visual fictions of the African continent than photography.[130]

OKWUI ENWEZOR AND OCTAVIO ZAYA

The art form formerly known as photography is finally being taken seriously in Britain,[131] but its roots in Africa are long and deep. The Photography Biennale held in Bamako, Mali is among the most important celebrations of contemporary photography in the world, and contemporary African photography was one of the main themes at the fifteenth Paris Photo Fair in 2011. However, this chapter is not concerned with the growing reputation of African photographers as artists of great talent, though that will, I hope, become evident from some of the images included in this book. My main concern here is to give an insight into how a knowledge and understanding of African textiles has been deepened by the way in which they have been recorded by photographers (African and non-African alike) since the mid nineteenth century, while at the same time being aware of the deceptions which the lens is more than capable of creating.

Very few textiles more than 150 years old, from any part of Africa, survive in museum collections – from certain regions, particularly coastal eastern Africa, virtually none. There are some obvious reasons for this, including the vulnerability of woven materials of various types to climate, insects and, of course, continuous use. Another reason involves the value judgements made by early collectors in Africa, whose interests lay mainly in works that were representative of the sculptural traditions which were deemed to be closest to Western ideals of 'high art'. Finally, ideas about what constitutes the 'real' Africa, still powerfully alive today, tended to exclude any works of art which had connections outside the continent – and inevitably militated against collecting many of the dynamic, cosmopolitan, yet distinctively 'African' traditions which I have highlighted in this book. In these circumstances, early photography often provides the only visual record of some of the magnificent cloths from which familiar contemporary African textile traditions sprang.

From the mid nineteenth century a large number of photographers began to operate in all parts of Africa, many of them itinerant, others setting up portrait studios in the rapidly expanding towns and cities of the continent. Until quite recently it was assumed that these early photographs were almost all produced by foreign rather than by local African photographers. However, ongoing research reveals a rather different picture. Many early photographers, such as N. Walwin of Accra, Ghana, J. A. C. Holm of Lagos, Nigeria and A. Lisk-Carew of Freetown, Sierra Leone, who were previously assumed to be European, were in fact African.[132] Even the prolific output of the Bonny-Opobo based photographer J. A. Green was not sufficient to reveal his African identity, as his full name – Jonathan Adagogo Green – would clearly have done.[133] In eastern Africa, many early photographers came from India, particularly from Goa, as well as from Europe, though further research may reveal an African authorship to works by 'unidentified photographers'. As I have shown elsewhere in this book, dress can be a powerful means of rebellion and of empowerment, two elements which come across very strongly in many early photographs from eastern and southern as well as from West Africa. The expressions on the faces of southern and eastern African people, particularly women, which appear in many of the images by 'unidentified photographers' are proud, yet engaged with the person taking the picture, which suggests to me that these photographs may be the work of local African photographers – as the author Olu Oguibe has pointed out, 'even in the face of opposition and active discouragement, Africans nevertheless took possession of the camera and photographic processes'.[134]

These early innovators in the art of studio photography paved the way for the great late-modernist photographers such as Seydou Keïta (see pp. 220–1) and Malick Sidibé (pp. 210 and 224) in Mali, and other less well-known talents such as Oumar Ly in Senegal (p. 223) and Jacques Touselle in Cameroon (p. 222), working in the decades before and immediately following independence. These photographers used a combination of textiles – as worn by their sitters and in the backdrops and other props featured in the pose – as integral elements in the composition of their work. The tension between the human subjects and the woven, printed, resist-dyed and embroidered landscape in which they appear creates a unique drama out of what otherwise might have been a series of simple studio portraits. The gradual decline in demand for studio photography in the 1980s forced a change in the use of the studio milieu by Samuel Fosso in the Central African Republic. Fosso used his own body, in the guise of a variety of personae, as a means of examining a range of subjects, from the legacy of colonialism to the machinations of the art world. Textiles frequently play an important role in Fosso's work, reflecting key characteristics of the stylized social types he portrays (see p. 225).

In Morocco and in their London and Boston studios, artist/photographers Hassan Hajjaj (p. 229) and Lalla Essaydi (p. 226) critique the often salacious and voyeuristic Western Orientalist tradition in painting and photography of the nineteenth and early twentieth centuries. In their different ways they mimic the composition of Orientalist images as a means of suggesting a way out of the stereotypical notions of North African culture – and of women's place in that culture – which these images had fostered in the Western imagination. Textiles are integral to the work of both artists, creating a kind of *trompe l'œil* effect by clothing their models in garments which at first sight seem to perpetuate Orientalist stereotypes, but which on closer inspection suggest a quite different and authentic world that challenges Western preconceptions on a very deep and fundamental level.

Textiles are not always used in the context of dress or clothing, as in the work of the South African artist Georgia Papageorge, who uses in her photographs great rivers of bright red cloth flowing across the landscape, or being carried in procession by hundreds of people (see p. 227). In this context cloth is used as a metaphor for drawing people together, whereas her use of chevron-patterned black-and-white cloth across the same landscape suggests the artificial barriers and divisions that drove people apart throughout the years of apartheid in her native South Africa. There are parallels here with the flamboyant colours worn by the *Sapeurs*, members of the *Societé des Ambianceurs et des Personnes Elégantes*,[135] a movement which began in Brazzaville, capital of the Republic of the Congo and which has recently been recorded by a number of photographers including the Congolese Baudouin Mouanda and the Italian Daniele Tamagni (see p. 231). These remarkable fashion statements have their roots in the ancient traditions of elaborate costumes and accessories worn by many of the peoples of the Congo River Basin, but they are also modern statements of emancipation from colonial rule and a determination not to succumb to the dictates of European codes of dress and colour, while at the same time overtly worshipping at the shrine of Parisian haute couture. They are also a joyous type of masquerade, in which the *Sapeurs* use cloth to transport themselves into a world beyond the drab reality of their impoverished urban surroundings.

'Makua Women',
unidentified photographer

These two women of the Makua people of northern Mozambique were photographed by an as yet unidentified photographer in the late nineteenth or early twentieth century. They wear strikingly patterned *capulanas* around their bodies and *lenço* (head-cloths), as well as the distinctive Makua nose ring. The cashew nut is a major source of income in eastern and southern Africa, nowhere more so than in Mozambique; the 'Paisley' pattern worn by the woman on the left became immensely popular because of its similarity to the shape of the cashew. Printed textiles in eastern and southern Africa, where slavery was not abolished until 1897, were worn as a sign of proud emancipation and increased freedom and personal prosperity.

'Women of Zanzibar', unidentified photographer

Two fashionable ladies from Zanzibar photographed in the late nineteenth or early twentieth century. The woman on the left wears a tailored dress, turban (*kilemba*) and trousers (*marinda*) favoured by the ruling elite of Arab descent on the island, though her shoeless feet immediately set her apart from that 'elite'. Her companion wears an early pair of *kangas* in a style which would become the distinctive dress of Swahili women from Somalia to south-east Africa. The bold, confident and united pose and expressions of the two women may have been an early statement of political, ethnic as well as social unity on Zanzibar, where such issues would be the source of discontent long after its union in the modern independent state of Tanzania.

Zanzibar, Chain-gang. Aug 25th 1896, unidentified photographer

These two famous photographs, apparently showing four enslaved African women with their 'Arab' slave driver, were taken by an unidentified photographer and inscribed with the title *Zanzibar, Chain-gang. Aug 25th 1896*. Although the East African slave trade was not officially abolished until 1897, these photographs are almost certainly posed, not least because the women are clearly fighting to keep their amusement under control. However, perhaps the greatest give-away is the clothing of the women. As the historian Laura Fair has pointed out:

During the early years of the twentieth century "Swahili" women also transformed their dress, abandoning items such as the dark kaniki *or cheap* merikani, *those badges of poverty and servility, in favour of the brightly coloured* kangas *(colourful, printed cotton cloths sold in pairs) imported from abroad ... Abandoning the clothing associated with slave status and adopting new clothing fashions was thus a highly symbolic act for women seeking to publicly pronounce their status as free women ... the makers and sellers of kanga were making a fortune off the women in Zanzibar who were said by many to be busily transforming their identities from those of slaves into "slaves of fashion".*[136]

The photographs are nonetheless a poignant reminder of the horrors of the slave trade, but at the same time providing the only record of some of the early designs of *kanga* with which women signalled their emancipation, including the pattern worn by the woman on the right which uses the famous carved wooden doors of Zanzibar as a recurring motif.

Kobena Gyan and his retinue, unidentified photographer

Kobena Gyan, a Fante king of Elmina on the coast of Ghana, and his retinue, photographed in 1894. Gyan had been exiled by the British to Sierra Leone in 1873, during the third Anglo-Asante war, for refusing to take an oath of loyalty, but returned in 1894 on the eve of the fourth Anglo-Asante war.[137] This photograph was undoubtedly taken to mark his reinstatement. The Fante had historically fought both for and against the British, mediating the balance of power between inland peoples such as the Asante and the Europeans on the coast. With one exception, Gyan and his entire entourage are dressed in printed cloth imported from Europe. The woman second from the right wears the characteristic narrow-strip cloth of the Ewe people. Her decision not to conform is probably accounted for by her position as a senior wife and is also a declaration of her Ewe identity.

Untitled portrait (below) and 'Fashion photo' for
Harper's Bazaar **(opposite) by Seydou Keïta**
Bamako, Mali, 1956–7 and 1998

The Malian photographer Seydou Keïta ran an enormously successful studio photography business in Bamako from 1948 until 1964. This image of a reclining woman was taken in 1956 or 1957. Keïta kept no records of his clients or when he took his photographs, later relying on the backdrops he used to roughly date his work. Much has been written about Keïta since his work was famously exhibited in New York in 1991,[138] but for the purposes of this book I am mainly interested in the ways in which textiles played such central roles – almost as characters in their own right – in his most powerful images. It was initially assumed that Keïta carefully selected the fabrics which his sitters wore or were photographed against or upon, very much in the way the European painters with whom he is sometimes compared would have done. In fact Keïta used the same backdrop and props for up to four years, and he admitted that 'sometimes the background went well with their clothes, especially the women, but it was all haphazard'. Haphazard or not, it was Keïta's genius as a photographer to dramatically juxtapose the 'constants' of his textile props – printed, woven or resist-dyed – with the 'variables' of the clothes in which his sitters arrived. Each sitting would last no longer than ten minutes, which meant that he had minimal time to make decisions, relying entirely on his eye to create images which are at once austere and opulent, restrained and exuberant.

In 1998 Keïta, by now a famous figure in the Western art world, did a fashion shoot in Bamako for *Harper's Bazaar*[139] (opposite). Once more he used textiles to create the image, but this time he had as much time as he wished, together with a much greater variety of textile props. While enchanting in their own right, these images perhaps highlight the reasons why his earlier portrait photographs have such an extraordinary power and intensity.

Two Friends **by Jacques Touselle**
Gelatin silver print
Mbouda, Cameroon, 1975

This superb portrait, simply entitled
Two Friends, was taken in 1975 by the
Cameroonian photographer Jacques
Touselle in his studio in the market town
of Mbouda. The matching printed textile
outfits they wear and the prestigious
objects they are holding, combined with
the backdrop of swirling drapes, draws
the pair together in a way which gently
emphasizes their joined hands at the centre
of the composition. I remember owning a
radio/cassette player in 1975 almost
identical to the one proudly displayed in
this photograph – I carried it with me a
great deal of the time because for the first
time it allowed me to listen and dance to
my favourite music where and when I
wished. The themes of wealth, modernity
and dancing are echoed in the electric fan
(*ventilateur*) which is the predominant
motif on the textiles they wear, and which
also alludes to a sexy dance of the same
name which was all the rage in West Africa
in the mid 1970s and remains popular
today (see p. 204). The question will
always remain as to whether the pair are
co-wives or sisters, or perhaps members
of a church choir or village community
group. These are the usual categories of
people who share cloth in this way in
Cameroon.

Portrait by Oumar Ly
Gelatin silver print
Senegal, 1970s

This portrait of a young woman was taken by
the Senegalese photographer Oumar Ly, probably
in the mid 1970s. The dress of printed fabric she
is wearing has been designed so that the
'bluebirds' that make up the predominant motif
are flying upwards in front and downwards
behind. This feature, together with the strong
vertical columns of the woven mat being held up
by Oumar Ly's assistant behind the subject, and
the angle at which the picture is taken, combine
to give an extraordinary sense of movement to
the composition.[140]

Vue de Dos by Malick Sidibé
Gelatin silver print
Bamako, Mali, 2001
60 x 60 cm

This photograph, *Vue de Dos*, was taken
in 2001. In the background hangs the
famous striped textile which forms the
backdrop to literally hundreds of Sidibé's
portraits of (mainly) young citizens of
Bamako over more than thirty years (see
p. 210). In this study, however, the sitter is
not gazing directly into the lens as in most
of Sidibé's portraits, but instead becomes
an element in an almost abstract
arrangement of striped Malian textiles.

Le chef: celui qui a rendu l'Afrique aux colons
(**'The chief: the one who sold Africa to the colonizers'**) **by Samuel Fosso**
C-print, from the series *Série Tati, autoportrait I–V*
Bangui, Central African Republic, 1997
145 x 102 cm

'With this photo I wanted to say to westerners, "Look, we had our own democracy before
you came, we had our own rulers, our own presidents, but it was our ruler that you came
and got rid of, and in his place you set up your hierarchies, your systems"'.[141] Thus Samuel
Fosso described his famous photograph. Textiles are an integral part of the image, from the
chief's faux leopard-skin outfit and the upholstery of his throne, to the cut-pile cushion which
keeps his divine feet from touching the floor and the huge, printed hand mirrors in which this
self-regarding despot admires himself. In part the image is a playful comment on the 'props'
which Fosso and most other studio portrait photographers in Africa would have made
available to their sitters, but it also pays laconic homage to the bargain-basement French
department store, Tati, in which any tin-pot dictator can find as much bling as he needs to
kit himself out for the job of ruling an African country – and all at knock-down prices.

From the series *Les Femmes du Maroc* by Lalla Essaydi, 2007 (AH 1427)

This image is profoundly different from that of Essaydi's close friend Hassan Hajjaj (see p. 229), but in some ways the two photographers are confronting similar issues. In this profoundly beautiful image the art of textiles, painting and photography seem to find a perfect balance. Essaydi says:

The preparations for the photo shoot start up to six months in advance, when I commence writing [in henna] on the fabric that covers the walls, the furniture and the women's clothing ... Henna is a crucial element in the life of a Moroccan woman. It is associated with the major milestones in her life and is a part of their celebration ... It takes more than six months to prepare enough fabric, for once the henna has dried, it flakes off easily ... I want the viewer to become sensitized to the voyeuristic, sexualized gaze of the Western Orientalist painters, but at the same time be enthralled with the authentic beauty of the culture these artists encountered in North Africa.[142]

Bloodlines and *Under the Banners*
by **Georgia Papageorge**
Lightjet photographs on Fuji Crystal
Archival paper
South Africa, 2008

The South African artist Georgia Papageorge
uses red cloth in much of her work,
sometimes as thin, jagged lines like a graph
cutting across her paintings, sometimes as
large swathes of cloth pouring out of the
crater of Mount Kilimanjaro, or cascading
like a waterfall down a cliff face in Brazil.
Papageorge calls them 'arterial lines',
symbolic of the blood which flows in the
veins of all people, no matter what the
colour of their skin. In this work the citizens
of two communities, Enon and Bersheba,
in the Eastern Cape, South Africa, formerly
divided by a fence during the years of the
apartheid regime, come together carrying
vast trains of red cloth. They met on July
10 2005 at a point where the fence stood,
thus symbolically healing the rift which
once divided the two communities.[143]

227

A New Beginning by Araminta de Clermont, Cape Town, South Africa, 2009–10

The British-born, South Africa based photographer Araminta de Clermont studied architecture before taking up photography, and her work is informed by an abiding interest in the relationship between the built environment and the people who appear in front of a backdrop of concrete and brick. This image of three young South Sotho men at a bus stop is part of the series *A New Beginning*, photographed between July 2009 and August 2010 in the townships surrounding Cape Town. The blankets which the men wear – and the way in which they wear them – have their origins in the animal skin cape, *kaross*, though their transition to factory-woven textile is credited to King Moshoeshoe I, who is also thought to have given his name to the indigo-dyed cloth *shweshwe* widely worn in South Africa today (see p. 102). Following a meeting between Moshoeshoe and the Scottish textile manufacturer Donald Fraser in 1876, the king reputedly negotiated the production of special blankets, which were not only more sturdy than the low-quality imported cloth which his people had taken to wearing, but which could also be worn in a way that more closely resembled the traditional skin *kaross*. Today a variety of blankets are worn by both men and women to signify rites of passage in Sotho society. When young South Sotho men prepare for transition to manhood they wear a certain type of blanket known as *moholobela* ('the fertility blanket'). These three young men wear another kind of blanket known as *lekhokolo*, which shows that they have completed the initiation ceremony and have reached manhood. Designs such as the maize cob or *Poone*, seen here on their *Seana Marena* label blankets, are very popular for *lekhokolo*, as they signify virility and fertility. De Clermont's poignant image shows the men at a bus stop, full of hope for the next part of life's journey, though in the background the township, to which they and their families have moved from rural Lesotho, spreads from horizon to horizon.

Seana Marena woven blanket
Wool and cotton
Made by Aranda Textile Mills (Pty) Ltd,
South Africa
165 x 155 cm
British Museum, 2012,2018.1

The *Seana Marena* (meaning 'king's blanket') with *Poone* (mealie/maize) design, signifying fecundity and prosperity, is reportedly most sought-after in the present colourway, i.e. blue, slate and black with vertical yellow/orange 'pin stripes'. Basotho blankets are now manufactured by Aranda in South Africa, although they were once imported from the UK. The history of the blanket worn by the South Sotho is thought to date back to the 1860s when an industrially made English blanket was presented to King Moshoeshoe I (*c.*1786–1870), founder of the kingdom of Lesotho.

Jama fna Angels by Hassan Hajjaj, 2000 (AH 1420)

These four ladies, dressed in animal print *djellabas* and Louis Vuitton slippers, their faces veiled, represent both the sexual fantasy and the nightmare which North Africa and the Middle East represents in the back alleys of the Western imagination. These are the 'Kesh Angels', the motorcycle-riding, football-playing babes of Marrakesh, with whom the London-based Moroccan artist/photographer Hassan Hajjaj playfully connives to subvert the stereotypes created by the Orientalism of the past century and the international fashion industry of the present day.

Advertisement and reality

During the Third Sansa workshop in 2009 (pictured right) organized by the Ghanaian artist Atta Kwami (see p. 61), the Iranian photographer Tooraj Khamenehzadeh took the two images below as part of a sequence of works examining the gulf between advertisements – in magazines, on bill boards, on TV – and the realities of life for women in the city of Kumase, Ghana. Beneath his own images he displayed crumpled and discarded advertisements, including one by the Dutch textile company Vlisco which manufactures many of the 'wax' print textiles that one of his subjects carries in a metal bowl on her head – and which she wears herself as a walking advertisement.

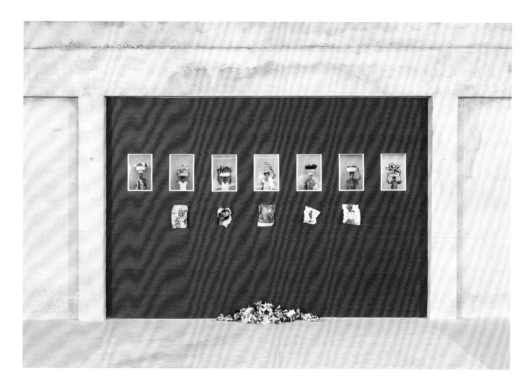

Sapeurs

A good deal has been written about the SAPE (*Société des Ambianceurs et Personnes Elégantes*) of Brazzaville and Kinshasa,[144] and in recent years the *Sapeurs*, brilliantly dressed African dandies, have attracted the attention of photographers such as the Italian photo-journalist Daniele Tamagni, and the Congolese Baudouin Mouanda. The history of the movement is sometimes traced to individual figures of the early twentieth century such as André Matsoua, an influential Congolese politician with a taste for French fashion in the 1920s. In fact, as has already been pointed out in Chapter Five, this region of Africa has a long history of trading in cloth, both imported and locally made, and dress has always played an important role in distinguishing various hierarchies in society. In a way the *Sapeurs* simply represent a recent manifestation of ancient traditions, though there is a real sense in which membership of this mutually supportive, though extremely hierarchical, society is almost an end in itself.

'Two members of the Piccadilly Group'
by Daniele Tamagni
Brazzaville, Republic of the Congo, 2007.

In his book *Gentlemen of Bacongo*, Tamagni describes how the Piccadilly Group was formed in 2001 by Ferol Ngouabi after seeing Prince Charles wearing a kilt. 'One of his [Ngouabi's] sisters living in the UK sends him original outfits, and already twelve out of the fifteen members of the Piccadilly Group wear a kilt.' According to one member, 'British people are very elegant, and are advanced in all aspects of life compared to other countries.'

Conclusion

Ny fihavanana ohatry ny landy: maty isika, ifonosana; velona, itafiana, ka ny madilana arahim-panondro.

'Friendship is like silk: it serves to wrap the dead, to dress the living, and when a thread is too thin, the finger follows it.'[145]

MALAGASY PROVERB

I began this book with four textile stories from global Africa and it seems right to draw it to a conclusion with four more stories which, although containing a 'global' element, attempt to look at the dynamism of ongoing traditions within the continent.

Textiles for marriage in Mahdia, Tunisia

The first comes from a small country in North Africa where a poor vegetable seller, Mohamed Bouazizi, set fire to himself in despair at the abuse of his human rights and personal dignity, and by so doing began what in Tunisia became known as The Dignity Revolution, though the global media dubbed it The Jasmine Revolution. In the disturbances that followed the ousting of President Ben Ali, I heard with sadness that Tunis railway station had burned down, probably at the hands of pro-Ben Ali supporters. It was there that Julie Hudson and I, on our first evening in Tunisia, had witnessed the 'event' master-minded by the artist Nja Mahdaoui (see pp. 68–9), and I can still see in my mind's eye his vast calligraphic patterned banners hanging at one end of the concourse. From that railway station we took a train south to the town of Mahdia, and it is there that this story unfolds.

The coastal town of Mahdia gets its name from 'Ubayd Allah, the self-styled Mahdi (literally 'the rightly guided one') who in AD 909 overthrew the Aghlabids and founded the Fatimid dynasty with its capital at Mahdia. 'Ubayd Allah is one of several figures in Islamic African history who have claimed to be the Mahdi, the most celebrated being Muhammad Ahmad, who founded the Mahdist state in northern Sudan in the late nineteenth century (see pp. 42–3).

For 600 years Mahdia was one of the most formidable fortified naval bases in the Mediterranean, though it later became famous for its weaving industry. Today weaving is still carried out in houses and small workshops within the medina in the Old Town, producing garments not only for the people of Mahdia but also, in different designs and colours, for other Tunisian towns such as Ksour Essaf, Chebba, Moknine, Bekalta, El Djem, and even beyond this region as far to the south as Gabes. In recent years a massive holiday development has sprung up around the Old Town, and there is no doubt that weavers supplement their incomes by selling to the passing tourist trade, though the majority of their custom comes from local people commissioning fine textiles to be worn at important ceremonies, particularly marriage.

When we visited Mahdia in 1998 much of the weaving and embroidering of fine garments was controlled by the Arousse family,[146] and I understand that little has changed in that respect. The master weaver, Karim el-Arousse, employed a dozen or more weavers who worked in several small ateliers using variants of the treadle loom, each designed to produce a particular type of cloth. Looms with four sets of heddles are used to weave the various belts worn as part of the ceremonial dress of women in Mahdia and in other towns such as Moknine and Ksour Essaf. A smaller variation of the belt-weaving loom, equipped with eight sets of heddles, is used to weave the silk headband (*kishf*) worn at marriage by the women of Mahdia. It is woven in a single-width strip, which is folded four times to form a narrow band, then hand-stitched together.

Much of the vigour of the textile traditions of Mahdia comes through the embellishment of woven cloth with embroidery and the addition of fringes, tassels, and pom-poms. In Mahdia, only women do this work on female dress, although men embroider items of male clothing such as the hooded gown (*burnous*) and tunic (*jibba*). The women embroiderers of Mahdia were also employed by Karim el-Arousse, but they work from their homes in the medina and take a great pride in their creations. Using an embroidery frame (*gorgaf*) they embroider the women's waistcoats (*farmala*) and head-veils (*khayatiya*) that are part of the marriage outfit.

Belts are woven in a mixture of wool and silk as a single piece of cloth with two distinct sections, each with a separate pattern and colour. They are then

cut up by the women embroiderers, placed together as three separate widths, with different pattern and colour front and back, then sewn together again using twisted yellow silk thread.

The two most prestigious silk cloths for marriage, *rida' ahmar* (see p. 171) and *rida' harir*, are woven in Mahdia. *Rida' harir* has weft bands of red, gold and blue silk and of silver and gold metallic thread at each end and a two-tone blue/red central section. The elaborate geometric motifs throughout the cloth are known as *khwatim tarabulsiy* ('Tripolitanian seal') and are achieved through the use of numerous shed sticks (*baguettes magiques*) inserted through the warp. Similar cloths are woven in Mahdia for the town of Chebba, but without silver bands, and for Gabes, but with *khwatim tarabulsiy* in two-tone red/green.

Female embroiderers also make and attach the tassels and fringes to other vital elements of the marriage costume such as the tunic (*qmajja tawaliy*) (see p. 47) and the belt (*hizem*). The *qmajja tawaliy* is a white cotton dress with black-work embroidered bodice, embellished with *hashiya* silk strips of complex pattern and fringed with tassels of green, orange, and red silk around the arms and hem. The trousseau of a young bride would contain twenty or thirty of

Above left **Marriage cloth (*rida' harir*) (detail)**
Silk
Mahdia, Tunisia, late 20th century
124 x 435 cm
British Museum, Af1997,04.4

Above right **Woman's square head-veil (*khayatiya*)**
Orange silk embroidered with flat, gold-covered thread known as 'till'
Mahdia, Tunisia, 1998
91 x 89 cm
British Museum, Af1998,01.68

The floral motifs on this piece include the jasmine, Tunisia's national flower.

these dresses, seven of which are worn, one on top of the other, on the 'night of henna' immediately prior to the marriage ceremony.

Karim el-Arousse had been researching the old patterns once used by weavers in Mahdia and had woven samples with colour combinations quite unlike anything else his workshops produce. Karim was modest about his achievement, but clearly excited about its potential, not only as a way of expanding his business into a new market and of satisfying his own creativity, but at the same time remaining true to what he undoubtedly saw as his responsibility in maintaining historical but dynamic and vital textile traditions in Mahdia, traditions worthy of Tunisia's Dignity Revolution.

Below left Weaving the silk marriage cloth (*rida' harir*). Atelier of Karim el-Arousse, Mahdia 1997.

Below right Mahdia wedding costume including silk head-veil (*khayatiya*) held in place by a head-band (*kishf*) and marriage cloth (*rida' harir*). Mahdia, 1998.

Silk textiles of the Merina, Madagascar

The patterned, nineteenth-century silk textiles of Tunisia are occasionally mistaken for those of the Merina kingdom of Madagascar, and although both countries have numerous and diverse textile traditions, only recently have they begun to be documented in detail. Through textiles past and present it is possible to read and reveal the diverse historical influences which have shaped cultures over many centuries. In Madagascar the names associated with different types of weaving are eloquent reminders of the Indian, Arabian, Swahili and Indonesian influences which have been assimilated into the fabric of Malagasy society. The innumerable textile-related sayings and proverbs of Madagascar reveal how central cloth is to the lives of Malagasy people:

> *In Madagascar, as elsewhere, proverbs reflect beliefs and attitudes regarding nearly all aspects of life. Proverbial expressions concerning cloth – especially the* lamba *and its uses – or employing textiles and clothing as metaphors are common in Madagascar. This stands to reason as in*

Patterned cloth (*lamba akotofahana*)
Merina people, Madagascar,
early 20th century
276 x 174 cm
British Museum, Af1949,10.1,
donated by James Keeves

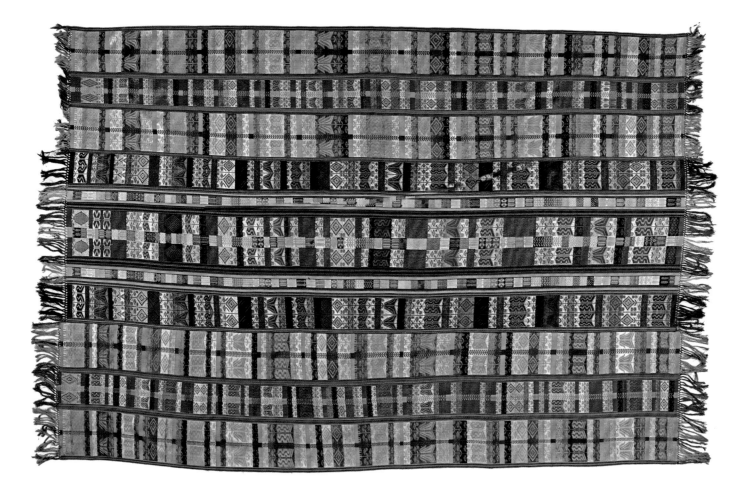

Malagasy culture, the act of dressing is expressive of
wisdom, and only those who have lost their abilities
to reason 'separate themselves from their clothes'
(manary lamba).[147]

The proverb with which this chapter opened is a beautiful
and subtle metaphor for the close relationship between people
and cloth: 'Friendship is like silk: it serves to wrap the dead, to
dress the living, and when a thread is too thin, the finger
follows it.' The somewhat enigmatic reference to the finger
relates to the process of reeling silk from a silk worm's cocoon,
which, like friendship, requires a steady and consistent motion.
If the thread of friendship is becoming too thin, the finger
thickens it by teasing out a little more silk. 'Wrap the dead' is a
reference to the silk burial cloth (*lamba mena*), literally 'red
cloth', woven from *landibe*, 'the little silkworm', indigenous to
Madagascar. In common with the *rida' ahmar*, 'red shawl', of
Tunisia (see p. 171), 'red' in this context does not necessarily
refer to the colour of the cloth itself, but more to the context in
which it is used, and thus to the symbolic associations of red in
Madagascar with power, authority and the ancestors. 'Dress
the living' refers to the numerous silk textiles, the most
spectacular of which are the elaborately patterned *lamba
akotofahana* woven from *landikely* ('the big silkworm',
Bombyx mori) which, together with the mulberry trees on
which they feed, were imported to Madagascar on the orders
of King Radama I in the early nineteenth century.[148]

Despite the extraordinarily complex patterning of these silk
cloths, they would have been woven on the comparatively
simple, fixed heddle ground loom as depicted by the artist
Rainimaharosoa (see above). During elaborate 'second-burial'
rituals (*famadihana*) – which, like much else in Malagasy
culture, have their origins in Indonesia – the Merina nobility
would not only be wrapped in the *lamba mena* noted above,

Merina woman weaving on a single heddle loom.
Painting by the Malagasy artist Rainimaharosoa, 1907.

Left **Lamba akotofahana woven by a member of the Merina revivalist weaving group Lamba SARL**
Silk
Arivonimamo, Madagascar, late 20th century
232 x 115 cm
British Museum, Af1993,14.1

A revivalist weaver of the group Lamba SARL.

but also in an additional shroud composed of a *lamba akotofahana*.

Only in the 1930s and 1940s were more complex treadle looms introduced by the French colonial authorities in an attempt to reproduce some of the patterns of nineteenth-century cloths which were preserved in the Queen's Palace Museum in the capital Antananarivo. Tragically, all of these nineteenth-century cloths, together with original paintings by Rainimaharosoa, were destroyed in the devastating fire of 6 November 1995, though if it is possible to see any positive outcome of this disaster, it might be that the rebuilding of the Museum has added impetus to an undoubted revival of Merina identity and cultural pride.[149]

When the Malagasy monarchy and the Merina kingdom lost power and authority during the colonial period, the significance of the colour and patterning of the *lamba akotofahana* dwindled, though the complex patterns continued to be woven into plain white cloths. During the nineteenth century,

Opposite **Patterned cloth (*lamba akotofahana*)**
Silk
Merina people, Madagascar, late 20th century
228 x 60 cm
British Museum, Af1985,17.1

the colour white generally signified lack of authority and had been worn largely by commoners and slaves. Despite this, some magnificent *lamba akotofahana* had been woven white-on-white for the Merina royalty and nobility in the nineteenth and early twentieth centuries, though in those contexts white took on its secondary significance of 'cooling, protective and non-aggressive qualities'.[150]

In recent years, and inspired by an exhibition of the arts of Madagascar at the British Museum in 1987, a group of Merina weavers named *Lamba* SARL was formed, with the support of the British art historian Simon Peers, in order to revive many of the lost weaving techniques of the nineteenth century Imerina kingdom[151] (see p. 239). Inspired by the success of this nucleus of weavers, and by a resurgent pride in Merina identity, a growing number of men and women are taking up the profession of weaving, using a variety of materials and colours to produce cloths which are taking Merina textile traditions in new and inventive directions.

Tartan cloth in Eastern and Southern Africa

For those not aware of the long tradition of Maasai warriors from Kenya and Tanzania wearing tartan patterned blankets, the cloth sold to visitors in the National Museums of Kenya's shops in 2006 must have come as a bit of a surprise, especially when they read the slogan written on the appliqué panel in the centre of

Tartan cloth with appliqué panel (detail)
Wool, cotton
Nairobi, National Museums of Kenya, 2006
150 x 195 cm
British Museum, 2011,2019.1

Maasai warriors wearing tartan blankets.

the cloth: NATIONAL MUSEUMS OF KENYA – WHERE TRADITION LIVES ON. Yet for me this textile perfectly captures some of the themes of this book – just as other countries and continents have assimilated 'African' textile patterns and colours, from London Transport upholstery to Paris haute couture, so African people, over the centuries, have taken imported textiles and turned them into traditions of their own. I particularly like the NMK textile (p. 240), because the logo which appears above the slogan on the central panel is of the two famous seventeenth-century Swahili side-blown horns, *siwa*, from Lamu and Pate islands on the north coast of Kenya. The image therefore combines a popular notion of tradition with one that makes the viewer stop and think.

A different use of tartan cloth may be observed among the followers of the Nazareth Baptist Church, *ibandla amaNazaretha*, founded in 1910 by the Zulu-Hlubi itinerant preacher and healer Isaiah Shembe at Ekuphakameni, 'the exalted place', close to the city of Durban on the eastern coast of South Africa. Today it is the largest African Initiated Church in South Africa, arguably in the entire continent, with a membership well in excess of one million. The church offers a calendar of events, a ritual cycle which ranges from mass gatherings to local congregations and intimate services held in individual homes. Shembe rituals, including an extraordinary variety of dances for men and women at various stages of their lives, are a syncretic mixture of Zulu and Christian belief, with a strong emphasis on the sacredness of dreams and visions. Each of the dances and ritual events is marked by the wearing of 'uniforms' governed by a strict dress code. During much of its existence the Shembe church and its leaders Isaiah, Galilee and Amos Shembe have had to struggle for survival and acceptance against a backdrop of colonial and apartheid regimes, and under the suspicious gaze of political and ecclesiastical officialdom, which may be one reason why followers of the church, in addition to Zulu beadwork and animal skin dress, also adopted tartan cloth and accessories such as umbrellas in their dance regalia.

Young girls returning from a communal gathering or 'camp', Nthanda. They wear the uniform known as *iskotch* for the sacred dance performances that take place after Nthanda. The umbrellas they carry signify rain – and thus fertility.[152]

The uniform known as *iskotch*, which includes the wearing of tartan kilts by both young men and virgin girls, dates back to the first decades of the Nazareth Church. It was worn at the funeral of Isaiah Shembe in 1935 and the tradition was enthusiastically continued by Isaiah's son Johannes Galilee Shembe. A photograph taken of Galilee Shembe in the 1930s[153] shows him wearing a tartan kilt, pith helmet and a uniform similar to those worn by Scottish soldiers during the colonial period and at battles of the Anglo-Zulu war such as Ulundi in 1879 – the Zulu word for tartan kilt and Highland soldier is the same – *umabubane*.[154] Today, young Nazarite men wear a similar ensemble of helmet, kilt and boots for the 'Scotch' dance. Kilts and red blouses are worn by girls in combination with beadwork ornaments on arms, knees and hands. They also carry umbrellas, another innovation by Isaiah Shembe, which relates to the ancient ceremony of *ukukhipa izinkomo* in which virgin girls, armed with spear and small shield, would take the cattle out to graze in a deliberate inversion of tasks strictly reserved for men. Shembe's philosophy of non-violence insisted on the substitution of umbrellas for spears.[155]

The reasons for the adoption of tartan kilts by the Shembe Church are complex and various, and have been discussed at length by scholars such as Robert Papini, Carol Muller and others.[156] The Scotsmen who came to South Africa as missionaries, and particularly as soldiers, were seen not only as colonizing, conquering and evangelizing foreigners, but also as outsiders who had been conquered and colonized themselves. The adoption of the Scottish kilt and other European dress and accessories may therefore have represented both concession and rebellion.

New African fashion

In 2006 I was lucky enough to see the fashion show by the great Senegalese designer Oumou Sy held at the Meticassana Café in Dakar during the Biennale (see p. 244). The show was a tribute to the intellectual and cultural theorist Leopold Senghor, the first president of independent Senegal, but Oumou Sy's collection was themed around the elaborate costumes worn by powerful and wealthy women of high status known as *signares* in eighteenth- and nineteenth-century Senegal.[157] I have to confess that I had never heard of the *signares* before that time, and Oumou Sy's creations opened a window onto a period of

Senegalese history which was both fascinating and horrifying, because the *signares* were closely associated with the Atlantic slave trade and were often the wives of European traders, or the daughters of such liaisons.

The winner of many awards and honours, Oumou Sy and other African fashion designers, from the Algerian-born Yves Saint Laurent onwards, have paved the way for a younger generation of designers who are now making their mark on the global stage. In her book *New African Fashion*, Helen Jennings states that 'Africa is fashion's new frontier'.[158] Well, yes and no. Africa and African textiles have been the inspiration for much Western fashion and design for more than a century – as I hope was clear in the Introduction to this book – and of course for Africans, with centuries of their own highly sophisticated fashion behind them, Europe and the West has been 'fashion's new frontier' for many years. However, there is no doubt that fashion designers of African heritage are now taking their rightful place as the creators of the most original and inspirational collections in the world. I am therefore proud to close this bookwith the work of the multi-award winning, London/New York based, Nigerian born designer Duro Olowu, pointing the way towards the African textiles of tomorrow.

Above Oumou Sy (with microphone) at the Meticassana Café, Dakar, 2006.

Left Image of a *signare* from the book by Abbé Boilat *Esquisses Sénégalaises*, 1853.

Opposite 'My intention was to create a freestyle, chic wardrobe for an independent spirit.'
Duro Olowu, 2011[159]

SIGNARE.

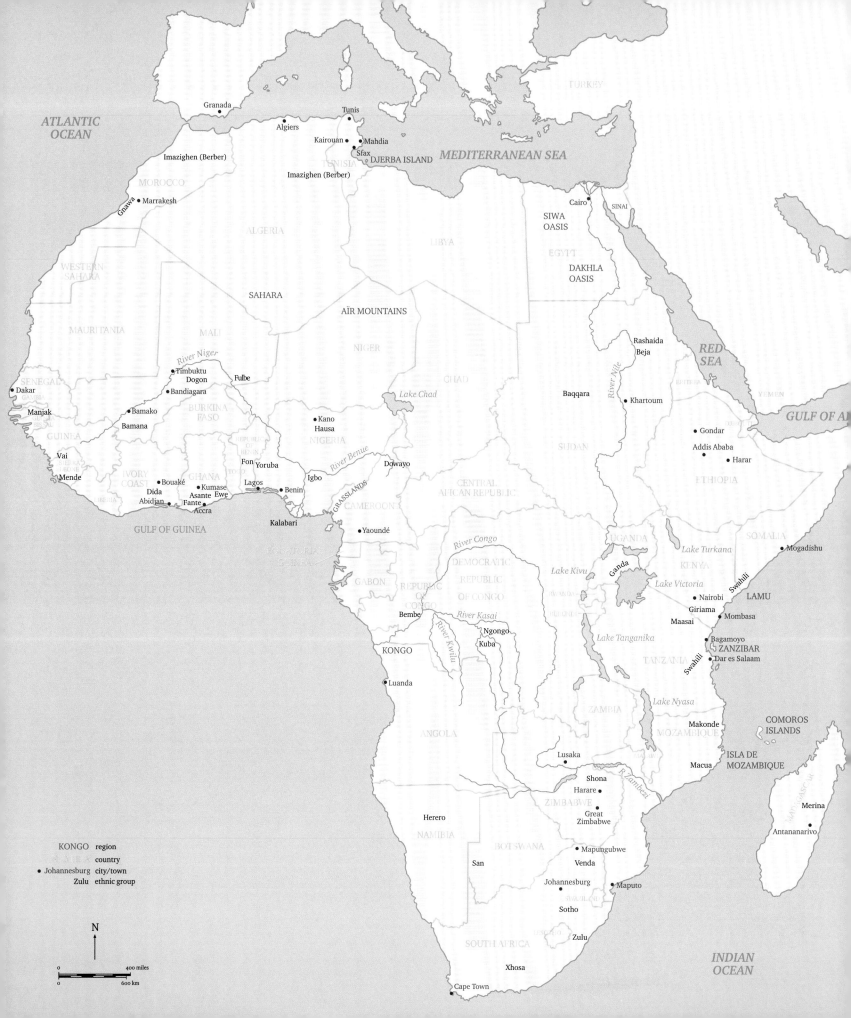

ATLANTIC
OCEAN

Granada

Tunis

Algiers

Kairouan • • Mahdia
Sfax
DJERBA ISLAND

MEDITERRANEAN SEA

TURKEY

Imazighen (Berber)

MOROCCO

TUNISIA

Imazighen (Berber)

Gnawa • Marrakesh

Cairo

SINAI

SIWA
OASIS

WESTERN
SAHARA

ALGERIA

LIBYA

EGYPT

DAKHLA
OASIS

SAHARA

RED
SEA

MAURITANIA

MALI

AÏR MOUNTAINS

NIGER

River Niger

Rashaida
Beja

River Nile

• Timbuktu
Dogon
• Bandiagara

Fulbe

CHAD

Lake Chad

Baqqara

• Khartoum

YEMEN

GULF OF A

SENEGAL

• Dakar

GAMBIA

Manjak

• Bamako
Bamana

BURKINA
FASO

• Kano
Hausa

NIGERIA

SUDAN

• Gondar

Addis Ababa •
• Harar

GUINEA-
BISSAU

GUINEA

Vai

SIERRA
LEONE

Mende

IVORY
COAST

LIBERIA

Dida
Abidjan

• Bouaké
• Kumase
Asante
Fante
Accra

GHANA

TOGO

Fon
Ewe

Yoruba
Lagos

Benin

Igbo

River Benue

Dowayo

ETHIOPIA

REPUBLIC
OF
BENIN

CAMEROON

GRASSLANDS

CENTRAL
AFRICAN REPUBLIC

Kalabari

GULF OF GUINEA

• Yaoundé

EQUATORIAL
GUINEA

River Congo

UGANDA

Lake Turkana

SOMALIA

• Mogadishu

GABON

DEMOCRATIC
REPUBLIC
OF CONGO

Lake Kivu

Ganda

Lake Victoria

KENYA

• Nairobi

Swahili

LAMU

REPUBLIC
OF
CONGO

River Kasai

Bembe

RWANDA

BURUNDI

Giriama
Maasai

• Mombasa

Ngongo
Kuba

Lake Tanganika

• Bagamoyo
ZANZIBAR

KONGO

River Kwilu

TANZANIA

Swahili

• Dar es Salaam

• Luanda

ANGOLA

ZAMBIA

Lake Nyasa

Makonde

COMOROS
ISLANDS

MOZAMBIQUE

ISLA DE
MOZAMBIQUE

• Lusaka

Macua

Shona

R. Zambezi

MADAGASCAR

Herero

• Harare

ZIMBABWE

Merina

NAMIBIA

Great
Zimbabwe

• Mapungubwe

BOTSWANA

Venda

• Antananarivo

KONGO   region

          country

• Johannesburg city/town

Zulu   ethnic group

San

• Johannesburg

SWAZILAND

• Maputo

Sotho

LESOTHO

N

SOUTH AFRICA

Zulu

INDIAN
OCEAN

Xhosa

0   400 miles

0   600 km

• Cape Town

Notes

1 Picton, J., 2002, 'Colonial pretense and African resistance, or subversion subverted: commemorative textiles in sub-Saharan Africa', in Enwezor, O. (ed.), *The Short Century: Independence and Liberation Movements in Africa 1945–1994*, Munich, London, New York, pp. 159–62.

2 Fair, L., 2001, *Pastimes and Politics; Culture, Community and Identity in Post-Abolition Urban Zanzibar, 1890–1945*, Athens, Ohio, Oxford, pp. 14–15, 103–8.

3 Picton, J. and Brown, C., (eds), 1995, *Textiles, Tradition and Lurex*, The Barbican Art Gallery, London.

4 Lagat, K. and Hudson, J., (eds), 2006, *Hazina: Traditions, Trade and Transitions in Eastern Africa*, The National Museum of Kenya, Nairobi.

5 Bortolot, A. I., 2007, *Revolutions: A Century of Makonde Masquerade in Mozambique*, The Miriam and Ira D. Wallach Art Gallery, New York, p. 22.

6 *New York African Burial Ground Archaeology: Final Report*, 2006, Chapter 10: 'The Coffins', pp. 272–74.

7 Tselos, S. E., 1996, 'Haitian Drapo Vodou: imagery, ritual and perception', in *Proceedings of the Fifth Biennial Symposium*, Textile Society of America, Inc., Illinois, pp. 58–67.

8 Mack, J., 1990, *Emil Torday and the Art of the Congo, 1900–1909*, London.

9 Siegmann, W.C., 2009, *African Art: A Century at the Brooklyn Museum*, Munich, Berlin, London, New York, pp. 11–27.

10 Fair, L., 2001, *Pastimes and Politics; Culture, Community and Identity in Post-Abolition Urban Zanzibar, 1890–1945*, Athens, Ohio, Oxford, pp. 80, 102–3.

11 Stoller, P., 2006, 'Trading places', in *Natural History*, Vol. III:6, July/August, pp. 48–55.

12 Rovine, V.L., 2004, 'Fashionable traditions: the globalization of an African textile', in Allman, J., (ed.), *Fashioning Africa: Power and the Politics of Dress*, Indiana, pp. 189–211.

13 Brett-Smith, S., 1982, 'Symbolic blood: cloths for excised women', in *Res*, Vol. 3, pp. 15–31.

14 Bolland, R., 1991, 'Tellem textiles: archaeological finds from burial caves in Mali's Bandiagara Cliff', *Medelingen van het Rijksmuseum voor Volkenkunde Leiden 27*, Amsterdam.

15 Weaver, C., 1989, 'Enid Marx: designing fabrics for the London Passenger Transport Board in the 1930s', in *Journal of Design History*, Oxford, Vol. 2, No.1, pp. 35–46.

16 Spring, C., 2008, *Angaza Afrika: African Art Now*, London, p. 186.

17 Spring, C., 2008, *Angaza Afrika: African Art Now*, London, pp. 34–7.

18 Bloomfield, S., 2010, *Africa United: How Football Explains Africa*, Edinburgh, p. 14.

19 Spring, C., 2005, 'Not really African? *Kanga* and Swahili culture', in Arero, H. and Kingdon, Z. (eds), 2006, *East African Contours: Reviewing Creativity and Visual Culture*, London, pp. 73–84.

20 Barlow, M., 2003, *El Anatsui 'Gawu'*, The Oriel Mostyn Gallery, Llandudno, p. 25.

21 Magnavita, S., 2008, 'The oldest textiles from sub-Saharan West Africa: woollen facts from Kissi, Burkina Faso', *Journal of African Archaeology*, Vol. 6, pp. 243–57.

22 Bolland, R., 1991, 'Tellem textiles: archaeological finds from burial caves in Mali's Bandiagara Cliff', *Medelingen van het Rijksmuseum voor Volkenkunde Leiden 27*, Amsterdam.

23 Spring, C. and Hudson, J., 1995, *North African Textiles*, London, pp. 49–52

24 Pacheco Pereira, D., (c.1506?), *Esmeraldo de situ orbis*, Lisbon, 1954, Vol. 3:2, p. 171.

25 Mack, J., 1990, *Emil Torday and the Art of the Congo, 1900–1909*, London, pp. 82–3.

26 Balicka-Witakowska, E. and Gervers, M., 1996, 'Monumental Ethiopian tablet-woven silk curtains: a case for royal patronage', *The Burlington Magazine*, Vol. 138, No. 1119, p. 379.

27 Torday, E., 1925, *On the Trail of the Bushongo*, London, p. 145.

28 Clarke, D., 2011, personal communication.

29 Gervers, M., 2004, 'The tablet-woven hangings of Tigre, Ethiopia: from history to symmetry', *The Burlington Magazine*, September 2004, CXLVI, pp. 597–9.

30 Spring, C. and Hudson, J., 1995, *North African Textiles*, London, pp. 99–104.

31 Ardouin, C., 2009, British Museum, Merlin database entry PRN EAF27364.

32 Spring, C. and Hudson, J., 2004, 'Urban textile traditions of Tunisia', *African Arts*, Vol. XXXVII, No. 3, Los Angeles, pp. 32–3.

33 Kriger, C. E., 2006, *Cloth in West African History*, Lanham, New York, Toronto, Oxford, p. 79.

34 Kriger, C. E., 2006, ibid., pp. 101–2.

35 Stephen Friedman Gallery., 2009, personal communication.

36 Nnenna Okore and Houghton, G., 2011, 'Metamorphic Processes: an interview with Nnenna Okore', in *Metamorphoses*, October Gallery, London.

37 Ogbechie, S. O., 2011, 'El Anatsui's intercultural aesthetics and the representation of Africa in global culture' in Kawaguchi, Y., (ed.), 2010, *A Fateful Journey: Africa in the Works of El Anatsui*, Osaka, pp. 38–9.

38 La Gamma, A. and Giuntini, C., 2009, *The Essential Art of African Textiles: Design Without End*, The Metropolitan Museum, New York.

39 Gumpert, L. (ed.), 2009, *The Poetics of Cloth*, The Grey Art Gallery, New York.

40 Barlow, M., 2003, *El Anatsui 'Gawu'*, The Oriel Mostyn Gallery, Llandudno.

41 Savage, P., 2006, 'Contexts, textiles and gin', in *El Anatsui: Asi*, David Krut/October Gallery, New York, London.

42 Okeke, C., 1994, 'Slashing wood, eroding culture: conversation with El Anatsui', *Nka: Journal of Contemporary African Art*, Issue 1, p. 37.

43 Storr, R., 2010, 'The shifting shapes of things to come', in Binder, L., (ed.), *El Anatsui: When I Last Wrote to You about Africa*, Museum for African Art, New York, p. 62.

44 Atta Kwami, 2006, *Statement of Work* by Atta Kwami, web.onetel.net.uk/~herbertroese/africa5.htm

45 Atta Kwami, 2006, ibid.

46 Owusu-Ankomah, 2006, in Melchers, J., (ed.) *Owusu-Ankomah Future Track*, Herzogenrath, p. 29.

47 El Salahi, I., 2000, in *Salahi*, Dara Art Gallery, Khartoum.

48 Spring, C. and Hudson, J., 1995, 'The patterns of life', *North African Textiles*, London, pp. 43–59.

49 El Anatsui, 2006, Kate McCrickard 'Telephone Interview', in: *El Anatsui*, David Krut/October Gallery, London, New York.

50 Atta Kwami, 2006, ibid.

51 Owusu-Ankomah, 2007, Artist's statement regarding work for the exhibition *From Courage to Freedom*, the October Gallery, London.

52 Issa, R., 1995, 'Nja Mahdaoui: a choreography of letters', in *Signs, Traces, Calligraphy: Five Contemporary Artists from North Africa*, London, Barbican Centre and Amsterdam, Tropenmuseum.

53 Cross, E., 2010, *Peterson Kamwathi: Matter of Record*, Ed Cross Fine Art, London.

54 Gbadamosi, R., 2009, 1. 'Laddade Färger' *Mana* No. 4–5; 2. 'What comes now', *Second Skins: Cloth and Difference*, INIVA, London.

55 Asemota, L., 2011, 'The Ens Project's first principles', *Exhibition Guide*, New Art Exchange, Nottingham.

56 Holmes, P., 2002, 'The empire's new clothes', Art News Online, October 2002.

57 British Museum, 2007, *Fabric of a Nation: Textiles and Identity in Modern Ghana*, A Partnership UK Project, London.

58 University of Ghana, Department Of Archaeology, 2007, *Fabric of a Nation: Textiles and Identity in Modern Ghana*, Legon.

59 Picton, J., 1995, 'Technology, tradition and lurex: the art of textiles in Africa', in Picton, J. and Brown, C., (eds), *Textiles, Tradition and Lurex*, Barbican Art Gallery, London, p. 29.

60 Picton, J., 1995, ibid., pp. 24–9.

61 Picton, J., 2002, 'Colonial pretense and African resistance, or subversion subverted: commemorative textiles in sub-Saharan Africa', in Enwezor, O. (ed.), *The Short Century: Independence and Liberation Movements in Africa 1945–1994*, Munich, London, New York, p. 160.

62 Rabine, L. W., 2002, *The Global Circulation of African Fashion*, Oxford, New York, pp. 135–68.

63 Picton, J., 2011, personal communication.

64 Yankah, K., 1983, *The Akan Trickster Cycle: Myth or Folktale?*, Indiana.

65 Glory, A. S., 2010, personal communication.

66 BBC World Service, 2000, *Kwame Nkrumah's Vision of Africa*.

67 Grover, P., and Morton, C., 2007, *Studio Cameroon: The Everyday Photography of Jacques Touselle*, Pitt Rivers Museum, Oxford.

68 Sule, G. O., 2011, personal communication.

69 Hamid, M. A., 1985, *Kanga*, Tanzania Media Women's Association, Dar Es Salaam.

70 Lieb Du Toit, J., 2005, 'Sourcing the use of indigo cloth in South Africa', in paper presented at the Design History Society, Metropolitan University, London.

71 Lieb Du Toit, J., 2005, ibid.

72 Lieb Du Toit, J., 2005, ibid.

73 Fair, L., 2001, *Pastimes and Politics; Culture, Community and Identity in Post-Abolition Urban Zanzibar, 1890–1945*, Athens, Ohio, Oxford, p. 64 ff.

74 Spring, C., 2005, 'Not really African? *Kanga* and Swahili culture', in Arero, H. and Kingdon, Z. (eds), *East African Contours: Reviewing Creativity and Visual Culture*, London, p. 75.

75 Lieb Du Toit, J., 2005, ibid.

76 Guille, J., 2010, personal communication.

77 Abdela, F., 1995, *The History of Kanga*, Zanzibar, p. 1.

78 Spring, C., 2005, ibid., p. 75.

79 Lieb Du Toit, J., 2005, ibid.

80 Papageorge, G., 2009, *Africa Rifting Bloodlines: Ceremonial Interactions 2001–2007*, Pretoria Art Museum, South Africa.

81 Hamdun, S., and King, N., 2005, *Ibn Battuta in Black Africa*, Princeton, pp. 15–16.

82 Odulate, T., 'Ankara, damask, lace and George – Nigerian or not?', 2009, *Esteem Wear Nigerian women's use of fabric*, http://www.xuu.org.uk/esteemwear/article1.html.

83 Stoller, P., 2002, *Money Has No Smell: The Africanization of New York City*, Chicago.

84 Vansina, J.,1998., 'Raffia cloth in West Central Africa, 1500–1800', in Mazzaoui, M. F., *Textiles: Production, Trade and Demand, An Expanding World: The European Impact on World History 1450–1800*, Vol. 12, Aldershot, Brookfield, Singapore, Sydney, pp. 263–81.

85 Pacheco Pereira, D., (c.1506?), *Esmeraldo de situ orbis*, Lisbon, 1954, Vol. 3:2, p. 171.

86 Vogt, J., 1975, 'Notes on the Portuguese cloth trade in West Africa, 1480–1540', in *International Journal of African Historical Studies*, Vol. 8:4, pp. 623–51.

87 Vogt, J., 1975, ibid., p. 636.

88 Spring, C. and Hudson, J., 1995, *North African Textiles*, London, p. 15.

89 Plankensteiner, B. and Adediran, N. M., 2011, *African Lace: A History of Trade, Creativity and Fashion in Nigeria*, Vienna, Lagos, Ibadan.

90 Aronson, L., 2001, '"We weave it:" Akwete weavers, their patrons, and innovation in a global economy', in Torntore, S. J., (ed.), *Cloth is the Center of the World: Nigerian Textiles, Global Perspectives*, Minnesota, pp. 17–28.

91 Renne, E. P., 2001, '"Our Great Mother . . . tied this cloth": *Pelete Bite* cloth, women, and Kalabari identity', in Torntore, S. J., (ed.), *Cloth is the Center of the World:*

Nigerian Textiles, Global Perspectives, Minnesota, pp. 29–41.

92 Spring, C. and Hudson, J., 2004, 'Urban textile traditions of Tunisia', in *African Arts*, Vol. XXXVII, No. 3, Los Angeles, pp. 38–40.

93 Menzel, B., 1990, 'Textiles in trade in West Africa', in *Textile Society of America: Symposium 'Textiles in Trade'*, Washington.

94 Labi, K. A., 2002, 'Fante Asafo flags of the Abandze and Kormantse: A discourse between rivals', in *African Arts*, Vol. XXXV, No. 4, Los Angeles, pp. 28–37, 92.

95 Abiodun, R., Beier, U., and Pemberton, J. III, 2004, *Cloth Only Wears to Shreds: Yoruba Textiles and Photographs from the Beier Collection*, Amherst, Massachusetts, p. 43.

96 Adams, M., 1978. 'Kuba embroidered cloth', in *African Arts*, XII, 1, pp. 24–39, 106.

97 Peers, S., 2004, 'History and change in the weaving of highland Madagascar', in Kusimba, C. M., et al (eds), *Unwrapping the Textile Traditions of Madagascar*, Field Museum and UCLA Fowler Museum, Los Angeles, p. 151.

98 Widman, R. W., 1967, *The Niombo Cult Among the Babwende*, Ethnographical Museum of Sweden, Monograph Series No. 11, Stockholm.

99 Spring, C. and Hudson, J., 2004, 'Urban textile traditions of Tunisia', *African Arts*, Vol. XXXVII, No. 3, Los Angeles, pp. 24, 28–31.

100 Cole, P. C., and Klemm, P. M., 2003, 'Historical threads: an overview of woman's dress in Harar', in *Archiv für Völkerkunde*, Vol. 53, pp 63–72.

101 Adams, M. and Holdcraft, T. R., 1992, 'Dida woven raffia cloth from Côte d'Ivoire', in *African Arts*, Vol. XXV, No. 3, Los Angeles, pp. 42–51.

102 Spring, C. and Hudson, J., 1995, *North African Textiles*, London, pp. 110–114.

103 Lamb, V. and Lamb, A., 1984, *Sierra Leone Weaving*, Roxford, pp. 150–55.

104 Lamb, V. and Lamb, A., 1981, *Au Cameroun: Weaving-Tissage*, Roxford, pp. 180–91.

105 McLeod, M. D., 1981, *The Asante*, London, pp. 107–111.

106 Spring, C., 2003, Unpublished field notes.

107 Heathcote, D., 1972, 'Hausa embroidered dress', Vol. V, No. 2, p. 14.

108 Spring, C. and Hudson, J., 1995, *North African Textiles*, London, pp. 43–59.

109 Bynon, J., 1984, 'Berber women's pottery: Is the decoration motivated?', in Picton, J. (ed.), *Earthenware in Africa and Asia*, London.

110 Spring, C. and Hudson, J., 2004, 'Urban textile traditions of Tunisia', in *African Arts*, Vol. XXXVII, No. 3, Los Angeles, pp. 34–41.

111 Gardi, B., 2009, (ed.), *Woven Beauty: The Art of West African Textiles*, Museum der Kulturen, Basel, p. 86.

112 Bowdich, T. E., 1819, *Mission from Cape Coast Castle to Ashantee*, London.

113 Kriger, C., 1988, 'Robes of the Sokoto Caliphate', *African Arts*, Vol. XXI, No. 3, Los Angeles, p. 52.

114 Heathcote, D., 1972, 'Hausa embroidered dress', Vol. V, No. 2, p. 18.

115 Spring, C. and Hudson, J., 2000, in Mack, J., (ed.) *African Arts and Cultures*, London, p. 52.

116 Wood, N. B., 2002, 'Shamans of Islam' in *Sacred Hoop*, Issue 38, pp. 23–4.

117 Spring, C. and Hudson, J., 1995, *North African Textiles*, London, pp. 99–104.

118 Papini, R., 2004, 'Dance uniform history in the Church of Nazareth baptists: the move to tradition', in *African Arts*, Vol. XXXVII, No. 3, Los Angeles, pp. 48–61, 90.

119 Barley, N., 1983, 'The warp and woof of culture', in RAIN, *Royal Anthropological Institute News*, No. 59.

120 Turner, V., 1982, *Celebration: A World of Art and Ritual*, National Museum of American Art, Washington D.C., p. 134.

121 Spring, C. and Hudson, J., 1995, *North African Textiles*, London, pp. 122–4.

122 Lefebvre, T., 1845–8, *Voyage en Abyssinie*, Paris.

123 Barley, N., ibid.

124 Aronson, L., 2001, '"We weave it:" Akwete weavers, their patrons, and innovation in a global economy' in Torntore, S. J., (ed.), *Cloth is the Center of the World: Nigerian Textiles, Global Perspectives*, Minnesota, p. 19.

125 Ramses Wissa Wassef Arts Centre, n/d, 'Threads of life: a journey in creativity', Harrania, Cairo, p. 6.

126 Bender, W., 2010, *Commemorative and other Cloths: Wolfgang Bender African Textiles Collection 2010*, 86, Unpublished notes.

127 Bender, W., 2010, ibid.

128 Tamagni, D., 2009, *Gentlemen of Bacongo*, London.

129 Cissé, K. and Gardi, B., 2009, 'Couvertures personnages', in Gardi, B., 2009, (ed.), *Woven beauty: The art of West African textiles*, Museum der Kulturen, Basel, p. 98.

130 Enwezor, O., and Zaya, O., 1996, 'Colonial imaginary, tropes of disruption: History, culture and representation in the works of African photographers', in Bell, C., (ed.) *In/Sight: African Photographers, 1940 to the Present*, Guggenheim Museum, New York, p. 20.

131 O'Hagan, S., 2011, 'British art takes photos seriously at last', *The Observer: The New Review*, 30.10.11, p. 38

132 Haney, E., 2010, *Photography and Africa*, London, p. 9.

133 Anderson, M. G., and Aronson, L. L., 2011, 'Jonathan A. Green: an African photographer hiding in plain sight', in *African Arts*, Vol. 44, No. 3, Los Angeles, p. 38.

134 Oguibe, O., 1996, 'Photography and the substance of the image', in Bell, C., (ed.), *In/Sight: African Photographers, 1940 to the Present*, Guggenheim Museum, New York, p. 233.

135 Friedman, J., 1994, 'The political economy of elegance: an African cult of beauty', in Friedman, J., (ed.) *Consumption and Identity*, Chur, pp. 167–87.

136 Fair, L., 2001, *Pastimes and Politics: Culture, Community and Identity in Post-Abolition Urban Zanzibar, 1890–1945*, Athens, Ohio, Oxford, p. 79.

137 Haney, E., 2010, *Photography and Africa*, London, p. 71.

138 Vogel, S., 1991, *Africa Explores: 20th Century African Art*, The Center for African Art, New York.

139 Bigham, E., 1999, 'Issues of authorship in the portrait photographs of Seydou Keïta', in *African Arts*, Vol. XXXII, No. 1, Los Angeles, pp. 56–67, 94.

140 Chapuis, F., and Pacaud, F., 2009, *Oumar Ly – portraits de brousse*, Paris.

141 Spring, C., 2008, *Angaza Afrika: African Art Now*, London, pp. 110–11.

142 Waterhouse, R., 2009., 'Lalla Essaydi: an interview', *Nka: Journal of Contemporary African Art*, No. 24, pp. 144–49.

143 Papageorge, G., 2009, *Africa Rifting/Bloodlines: Ceremonial Interactions 2001–2007*, Pretoria Art Museum.

144 'Gasworks: The Triangle Network', 2011, *Baudouin Mouanda*, www.gasworks.org. *See also* Friedman, J., 1994, ibid., and Gondola, C. D., 1999, 'Dream and drama: the search for elegance among Congolese youth', in *African Studies Review*, Vol. 42, No. 1, pp. 23–48.

145 Radimilahy, C., 2004, 'Lamba and proverbs', in Kusimba, C. M., et al (eds), *Unwrapping the Textile Traditions of Madagascar*, Field Museum and UCLA Fowler Museum, Los Angeles, p. 175.

146 Spring, C. and Hudson, J., 2004, 'Urban textile traditions of Tunisia', in *African Arts*, Vol. XXXVII, No. 3, Los Angeles, pp. 34–41.

147 Radimilahy, C., ibid., p. 174

148 Spring, C. and Hudson, J., 2002, *Silk in Africa*, London, p. 8.

149 Fee, S., 2002, 'Cloth in motion: Madagascar's textiles through history', in Kreamer, C. M., and Fee, S., *Objects as Envoys: Cloth, Imagery and Diplomacy in Madagascar*, National Museum of African Art, Smithsonian Institution, Seattle and London, p. 82.

150 Mack, J., 1989, *Malagasy Textiles*, Aylesbury, p. 44.

151 Fee, S., 2002, ibid., pp. 77–88.

152 Muller, C., 1999, *Rituals of Fertility and the Sacrifice of Desire: Nazarite Women's Performance in South Africa*, Chicago, p. 183.

153 Muller, C., 1999, ibid., pp. 119–20.

154 Papini, R., 2002, 'The Nazareth Scotch: dance uniform as admonitory infrapolitics for an eikonic Zion City in early Union Natal', in *Southern African Humanities*, Vol. 14, Pietermaritzburg, p.85.

155 Muller, C., 1999, ibid., p. 183.

156 Papini, R., 2002; Muller, C., 1999, ibid.

157 Boilat, Abbé P. D., 1853, *Esquisses Sénégalaises*, Paris.

158 Jennings, H., 2011, *New African Fashion*, Munich, London, New York p. 8.

159 Jennings, H., 2011, ibid., p. 20.

Further reading

Abiodun, R., Beier, U., and Pemberton, J. III, 2004, *Cloth Only Wears to Shreds: Yoruba Textiles and Photographs from the Beier Collection*, Amherst, Massachusetts.

African Arts (Quarterly journal), University of California, Los Angeles, 1967.

Akron Art Museum, 2010, *Pattern ID*, Akron, Ohio.

Allman, J., (ed.), *Fashioning Africa: Power and the Politics of Dress*, Indiana University Press, Indiana.

Arero, H. and Kingdon, Z. (eds), *East African Contours*, Horniman Museum, London, 2005.

Barlow, M., 2004, *El Anatsui 'Gawu'*, The Oriel Mostyn Gallery, Llandudno.

Becker, C., 2006, 'Amazigh textiles and dress in Morocco', in *African Arts*, Vol. XXXIX, No. 3, Los Angeles.

Bell, C., (ed.) *In/Sight: African Photographers, 1940 to the Present*, Guggenheim Museum, New York.

Binder, L., (ed.), *El Anatsui: When I Last Wrote to You about Africa*, Museum for African Art, New York.

Bolland, R., 1991, 'Tellem textiles: archaeological finds from burial caves in Mali's Bandiagara Cliff', in *Medelingen van het Rijksmuseum voor Volkenkunde Leiden 27*, Amsterdam.

Bowdich, T. E., 1819, *Mission from Cape Coast Castle to Ashantee*, London.

Bravmann, R.A., 1983, *African Islam*, Smithsonian Institution Press, Washington.

Coppard, A. (ed.), 2011, *Aware: Art, Fashion, Identity*, Royal Academy of Arts, London.

Dennis, A. B., 2004, *The Pride of Ewe Kente*, Accra.

Enwezor, O. (ed.), 2001, *The Short Century: Independence and Liberation Movements in Africa 1945–1994*, Munich, London, New York.

Faber, P., 2010, *Long Live the President: Portrait Cloths from Africa*, Tropenmuseum, Amsterdam.

Fair, L., 2001, *Pastimes and Politics; Culture, Community and Identity in Post-Abolition Urban Zanzibar, 1890–1945*, Athens, Ohio, Oxford.

Garb, T., 2011, *Figures and Fictions: Contemporary South African Photography*, Victoria and Albert Museum, London.

Gardi, B., 2009, (ed.), *Woven Beauty: The Art of West African Textiles*, Museum der Kulturen, Basel.

Gillow, J., 2001, *Printed and dyed Textiles from Africa*, British Museum Press, London.

Gumpert, L. (ed.), 2009, *The Poetics of Cloth*, The Grey Art Gallery, New York.

Hamdun, S., and King, N., 2005, *Ibn Battuta in Black Africa*, Princeton.

Haney, E., 2010, *Photography and Africa*, London.

Jennings, H., 2011, *New African Fashion*, Munich, London, New York.

Kawaguchi, Y., *A Fateful Journey: Africa in the Works of El Anatsui*, Osaka.

Koert, R. Van, 2007, *Dutch Wax Design Technology: From Helmond to West Africa*, Helmond.

Kreamer, C. M., and Fee, S., *Objects as Envoys: Cloth, Imagery and Diplomacy in Madagascar*, National Museum of African Art, Smithsonian Institution, Seattle and London.

Kriger, C. E., 2006, *Cloth in West African History*, Lanham, New York, Toronto, Oxford.

Kusimba, C. M., et al (eds), *Unwrapping the Textile Traditions of Madagascar*, Field Museum and UCLA Fowler Museum, Los Angeles.

La Gamma, A. and Giuntini, C., 2009, *The Essential Art of African Textiles: Design Without End*, The Metropolitan Museum, New York.

Lagat, K. and Hudson, J., (eds), 2006, *Hazina: Traditions, Trade and Transitions in Eastern Africa*, The National Museum of Kenya, Nairobi.

Lamb, V., 1975, *West African Weaving*, London.

Lamb, V. and Lamb, A., 1984, *Sierra Leone Weaving*, Roxford.

Lamb, V. and Lamb, A., 1981, *Au Cameroun: Weaving-Tissage*, Roxford.

Lieb Du Toit, J., 2005, 'Sourcing the use of indigo cloth in South Africa', Paper presented at the Design History Society, Metropolitan University, London.

Mack, J., (ed.), 2000, *African Arts and Cultures*, London.

Mack, J., 1986, *Madagascar, Island of the Ancestors*, London.

Mack, J., 1989, *Malagasy Textiles*, Aylesbury.

Mack, J., 1990, *Emil Torday and the Art of the Congo*, London.

Mazzaoui, M. F., 1998, *Textiles: Production, Trade and Demand, An Expanding World: The European Impact on World History 1450-1800*, Vol. 12, Aldershot, Brookfield, Singapore, Sydney.

Mcleod, M. D., 1981, *The Asante*, London.

Melchers, J., (ed.), 2006, *Owusu-Ankomah Future Track*, Herzogenrath.

Moore, E. aus dem, et al., 2009, *Prêt-à-Partager: A Transcultural Exchange in Art, Fashion and Sports*, Stuttgart.

Muller, C., 1999, *Rituals of Fertility and the Sacrifice of Desire: Nazarite Women's Performance in South Africa*, Chicago.

Njami, S et al., 2004, *Africa Remix: Contemporary Art of a Continent*, Hayward Gallery, London.

Papini, R., 2002, 'The Nazareth Scotch: dance uniform as admonitory infrapolitics for an eikonic Zion City in early Union Natal', in *Southern African Humanities*, Vol. 14, Pietermaritzburg.

Papini, R., 2004, 'Dance uniform history in the church of Nazareth baptists: the move to tradition', in *African Arts*, Vol. XXXVII, No. 3, Los Angeles, pp. 48–61, 90.

Perani, J and Wolff, N. H., 1999, *Cloth, Dress and Art Patronage in Africa*, Oxford, New York.

Picton, J. & Mack, J., 1989, *African Textiles*, London.

Picton, J. and Brown, C., (eds), 1995, *The Art of African Textiles: Textiles, Tradition and Lurex*, The Barbican Art Gallery, London.

Picton, J., 2002, 'Colonial pretense and African resistance, or subversion subverted: commemorative textiles in sub-Saharan Africa', in Enwezor, O. (ed.), *The Short Century: Independence and Liberation Movements in Africa 1945–1994*, Munich, London, New York, pp. 159–162.

Plankensteiner, B. and Adediran, N. M., 2011, *African Lace: A History of Trade, Creativity and Fashion in Nigeria*, Vienna, Lagos, Ibadan.

Rabine, L. W., 2002, *The Global Circulation of African Fashion*, Oxford, New York.

Relph, M. and Irwin, R., 2010, *African Wax Print: A Textile Journey*, Holmfirth.

Ross, D., 1998, *Wrapped in Pride: Ghanaian Kente and African-American Identity*, Los Angeles, Fowler Museum of Cultural History.

Rovine, V.L., 2004, 'Fashionable traditions: the globalization of an African textile', in Allman, J., (ed.), *Fashioning Africa: Power and the Politics of Dress*, Indiana.

Spencer, A. M., 1982, *In Praise of Heroes: Contemporary African Commemorative Cloth*, Newark Museum, New Jersey.

Spring, C. and Hudson, J., 1995, *North African Textiles*, London.

Spring, C. and Hudson, J., 2002, *Silk in Africa*, British Museum Press, London.

Spring, C. and Hudson, J., 2004, 'Urban textile traditions of Tunisia', in *African Arts*, Vol. XXXVII, No. 3, Los Angeles.

Spring, C., 1993, *African Arms and Armour*, British Museum Press, London.

Spring, C., 2005, 'Not really African? *Kanga* and Swahili Culture', in Arero, H. and Kingdon, Z. (eds), *East African Contours: Reviewing Creativity and Visual Culture*, London, Horniman Museum.

Spring, C., 2008, *Angaza Afrika: African Art Now*, London.

Stevenson, M. and Graham-Stewart, M., 2001, *Surviving the Lens: Photographic Studies of South and East African People, 1870–1920*, Vlaeberg.

Stone, C., 1985, *The Embroideries of North Africa*, Longman, London.

Tamagni, D., 2009, *Gentlemen of Bacongo*, London.

Torntore, S. J., (ed.), 2001, *Cloth is the Center of the World: Nigerian Textiles, Global Perspectives*, Minnesota.

Vansina, J.,1998., 'Raffia cloth in West Central Africa, 1500–1800', in Mazzaoui, M. F., *Textiles: Production, Trade and Demand, An Expanding World: The European Impact on World History 1450–1800*, Vol. 12, Aldershot, Brookfield, Singapore, Sydney, pp. 263–81.

Vogt, J., 1975, 'Notes on the Portuguese cloth trade in West Africa, 1480–1540', in *International Journal of African Historical Studies*, Vol. 8:4, pp. 623–51.

Widman, R.W., 1967, *The Niombo Cult Among the Babwende*, Ethnographical Museum of Sweden, Monograph Series No. 11, Stockholm.

Glossary

atelier workshop or studio.

adinkra **cloth** a traditional fabric of Ghana, patterned with symbolic designs hand-printed using stamps carved out of gourds. Each *adinkra* symbol has its own significance, representing a particular concept or proverb.

adinkrahene the head of the guild of *adinkra* carvers and cloth makers. Also the 'chief' *adinkra* symbol, a pattern of concentric circles representing greatness, charisma or leadership.

adire Yoruba word for resist-dyeing with indigo. *Adire* means to 'tie and dye'.

adire alabere see *adire oniko*

adire eleko Yoruba technique whereby designs are painted or stencilled on cloth using starch paste as the resisting agent.

adire oniko (also *adire alabere*) Yoruba tie-dyeing technique which uses raffia stitching or tying as the resist.

appliqué technique of stitching a supplementary piece of fabric on to a background cloth.

batik Javanese method of resist-dyeing using wax.

biskri ceremonial garment worn by the women of Djerba Island, Tunisia, initially at marriage. The name of the cloth is said to derive from the town of Biskra in Algeria, although it is unclear whether Algerian weavers settled on Djerba Island or if the cloth was introduced as a result of trade.

bogolanfini African discharge-dyed cloths of the Bamana people of Mali, often referred to as 'mud cloths'.

capulana printed wrap-around garment of Mozambique, often worn with a headscarf, *lenço*, and tailored blouse, *quimau*.

chechia a red, felted skull-cap; the traditional headwear of Tunisian men.

cheramine the printed cloth of the Comoros Islands.

cut-pile style of embroidery common among the Kuba peoples of the Democratic Republic of Congo. The technique involves taking raffia threads through the surface of raffia fabric and trimming them off close to the surface with a sharp blade to produce a velvety pile. Kuba cut-pile cloth is often referred to as 'Kasai velvet'.

draw loom a special type of loom that increases the capacity for weaving figured fabrics. The loom is operated by the weaver and one or more assistants who 'draw up' the supplementary heddles to form the pattern elements on a textile.

discharge-dye the process by which colour is removed from fabrics, usually by using a combination of river mud and caustic solution, to create a pattern.

guntino black and white or red and white printed cloth of Somalia. Unlike the *kanga*, the guntino is without images and inscriptions.

'Fancy' print a type of mechanically produced cloth. The designs on such cloths are produced without the aid of a resist agent, and on one side only. The introduction of the technique in the 1920s allowed for the reproduction of photographic images for the first time.

indigo blue dye obtained from various plants of the genus *Indigofera*. If indigo is to 'take', exposure to the air (oxidation) is necessary. Can also refer to the synthetic indigo-dye.

kanga a rectangular printed cloth sold and worn in matching pairs, principally by women in Tanzania, Kenya and other countries in eastern Africa. *Kangas* are, however, sometimes worn singly by Maasai men. Each *kanga* is printed with its own name and design. Similar printed cloths are the *capulana*, *cheramine*, *guntino* and *lenço*.

kente the narrow-strip hand-woven cloths of West Africa. The term is commonly used to refer to the silk narrow-strip cloth of the Asante and Ewe people in particular.

lamba the generic name for cloth in Madagascar.

lamba akotofahana silk cloth of complex pattern used by the nobility of the nineteenth-century kingdom of Imerina in Madagascar.

lamba hoany printed cloth of Madagascar, similar to the *kanga* in that it includes an inscription in Malagasy, yet it is worn by both men and women.

lenço headscarf or handkerchief.

quimau tailored blouse, often worn with a *capulana* and *lenço*.

resist-dye the process by which a textile is dyed using a resist substance (such as starch or wax) or technique (such as tying or stitching) to prevent dye from penetrating certain areas of a fabric. The technique is used to create a design in contrasting colours.

samakaka the printed cloth of the Herero people of Angola, a little like the *kanga* but without an inscription.

selvage (or selvedge) side edge of a fabric, where the weft returns – the non-fraying edge of a piece of cloth.

shed on a loom, the opening made between two layers of warp threads, through which the weft threads are passed.

shweshwe the term used by Sotho and Zulu speakers to describe discharge-printed indigo cloth. The cloth is known as *amajaman/ujamani*, or more recently *idark* among Xhosa speakers and *amotoishi* (in Pedi) and sometimes 'German print'.

Silk Road refers to a historical network of trade routes that connected eastern, southern and western Asia with Europe and parts of northern and eastern Africa.

trousseau the possessions, such as clothing and linens, that women, in some cultures, assemble for marriage.

warp threads that run lengthways in a fabric.

warp-faced a fabric in which the warp threads predominate over the weft (which is almost obscured).

wax-printing a design technique that involves using wax as a resist to prevent certain areas of fabric from accepting dye. The design is drawn in a dye-resistant substance known as a resist (such as a wax or paste), so that after dyeing it is still the same colour and stands out against the dyed areas.

weft the thread that is passed from selvage to selvage in a woven structure.

weft-faced term describing a fabric in which the weft completely covers the warp.

weft-inlay supplementary discontinuous weft forming blocks of inlay pattern.

Author's acknowledgements

My grateful thanks to all the artists, photographers, professional colleagues, friends and family who have generously contributed images, ideas, advice and encouragement in creating this book. In particular, I am deeply indebted to Hassan Hajjaj, Heidi Cutts and the late Dr. Katesa Schlosser for allowing me to use so many of their wonderful photographs in the book, and to El Anatsui, Samuel Fosso and Araminta de Clermont whose images appear on the cover and frontispiece.

A very big thankyou to my editor, Emma Poulter, who was highly professional but also great fun to work with, to my picture researcher Axelle Russo who went the extra mile in sourcing images from around the world, and to Mike Row for his expert photography of textiles in the BM's collections, assisted by Helen Wolfe, Cynthia McGowan and Catherine Elliott. Thanks also to Melanie Morris and Sheila McKenna from the British Museum Press for their input at crucial moments, and to Rosemary Bradley for her enthusiasm from the start of the project.

I thank friends and colleagues who read and commented upon various drafts of the text, including John Picton, Julie Hudson, Cynthia McGowan, Fiona Sheales and Lisa Galvin and in particular Catherine Elliott, whose expert and painstaking proofreading and constructive comments were invaluable. Love and thanks also to my wife, Yvonne Ayo, and to my children Will and Madeleine who had to do without me for lengthy periods, even when they didn't want to do without me!

There is too little space to mention by name all those who in one way or another helped with this book, but thank you all. However, I must thank the following, not only for allowing me to reproduce their wonderful work in this book, but also for their friendship and advice throughout:

Georgia Papageorge, Karel Nel, Gloria Ojulari Sule, Dr Zachary Kingdon, Luiz dos Santos, Rachid Koraïchi, Taslim Martin, Toby Clarke, Malick Sidibé, the late Seydou Keïta, Jacques Touselle, Oumar Ly, Peterson Kamwathi, Yinka Shonibare MBE, Katherine Coleman, Nnenna Okore, Wolfgang Bender, Raimi Gbadamosi, Abdoulaye Konaté, Atta Kwami, Ibrahim el Salahi, Owusu-Ankomah, Leo Asemota, Nja Mahdaoui, Lalla Essaydi, Tessa Jackson, Grace Ndiritu, Barbara Plankensteiner, Elisabeth Lalouschek, Akwele Suma Glory, Tooraj Khamenehzadeh, Daniele Tamagni, Simon Peers, Oumou Sy and Duro Olowu.

Picture credits

Every effort has been made to trace the copyright holders of the images used in this publication. All British Museum photographs are © The Trustees of the British Museum.

Page

4	© Araminta de Clermont
9 (*inset*)	© Chris Spring
11	© Dr Zachary Kingdon
12	© Chris Spring
14	© Luiz Santos
15 (*left*)	© Chris Spring
16	© Chris Spring
19 (*top*)	Photo Baron de Meyer; reproduced from *Textile: The Journal of Cloth & Culture*, 2006, Vol. 4, issue 6, p. 79
19 (*below*)	© Chris Spring
20 (*top*)	© Heidi Cutts
21 (*below*)	© The Conran Shop, London
22	© Taslim Martin
25 (*below*)	© Hassan Hajjaj
35	© The Trustees of the British Museum
38	© Toby Clarke
46 (*right*)	© Chris Spring
51	© the artist and courtesy of the artist and Stephen Friedman Gallery, London
52	© Nnenna Okore, courtesy of the October Gallery
61 (*below*)	© Katherine Coleman
65	© Abdoulaye Konate, courtesy of INIVA
69	© Chris Spring
73	© Chris Spring
74	© Heidi Cutts
77	© Heidi Cutts
79	© Heidi Cutts
83	Courtesy of Grace Ndiritu and LUX, London
90	© Photo Chris Spring with kind permission of Akwele Suma Glory

92	© Jacques Touselle
97	© Gloria Ojulari Sule
98	© Karel Nel
101	Courtesy of Grace Ndiritu and LUX, London
103 (*below*)	© Zanzibar Archive
104	© Chris Spring
108 (*right*)	© Zanzibar Archive
110	© Chris Spring
113 (*below*)	From unidentified photographer; © Natural History Museum, Maputo
114	© Chris Spring
115 (*left*)	© Dr Katesa Schlosser
117	© Georgia Papageorge
123	© Hassan Hajjaj
125	© Heidi Cutts
127	© Dr Katesa Schlosser
129 (*below*)	© Chris Spring
133	© Barbara Plankensteiner
137	© Chris Spring
144	© Chris Spring
147	© Julie Hudson
159	© Heidi Cutts
162–63 (*below*)	British Museum; © Fiona Sheales
163 (*top*)	© Gordon Frimpone
164	© Dr Katesa Schlosser
165	© Chris Spring
172 (*left*)	© Royal Geographical Society
172 (*right*)	© Chris Spring
177 (*below*)	© Dr Katesa Schlosser
183	© Hassan Hajjaj
191	© The Trustees of the British Museum
193	© Dr Katesa Schlosser

202	© Heidi Cutts
209	© Hassan Hajjaj
210	Courtesy of Magnin-A; © Malick Sidibe
216	From unidentified photographer, Maputo; © Heidi Cutts
217	© Zanzibar Archive
218	© Zanzibar Archive
219	Source: Library of Congress
220	Courtesy CAAC – The Pigozzi Collection, Geneva; © Seydou Keïta/IPM
221	Courtesy CAAC – The Pigozzi Collection, Geneva; © Seydou Keïta/IPM
222	© Jacques Touselle
223	© Oumar Ly, courtesy Galerie Les filles du calvaire
224	Courtesy Magnin-A; © Malick Sidibe
225	© Samuel Fosso, courtesy of Jean Marc Patras Galerie
226	© Lalla Essaydi
227	© Georgia Papageorge
228	© Araminta de Clermont
229 (*below*)	© Hassan Hajjaj
235	© Chris Spring
237	© The Trustees of the British Museum
239 (*right*)	© Simon Peers
241	Photographer Nigel Pavitt/Getty Images
242	© Dr Katesa Schlosser
244 (*top*)	© Myriam Louviot
244 (*below*)	© The Trustees of the British Museum
245	© John-Paul Pietrus/Art + Commerce/Fashion by Duro Olowu

Index

Page numbers in *italics* refer to illustrations

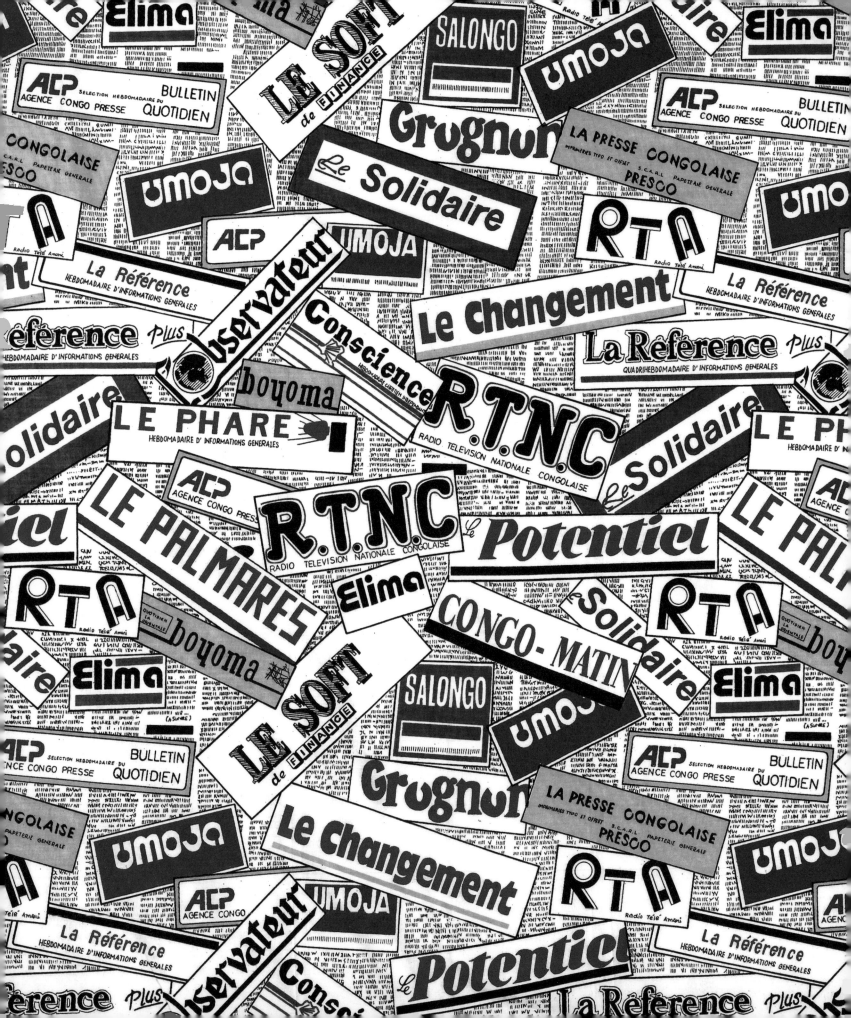